Audun Dybdahl
Ola Kai Ledang
Nils Holger Petersen (eds.)

GREGORIAN CHANT AND MEDIEVAL MUSIC

Proceedings from
The Nordic Festival and Conference
of Gregorian Chant
Trondheim, St. Olavs Wake 1997

Senter for middelalderstudier • Skrifter
Hovedredaktør: Senterleder Audun Dybdahl

Editions of SfMs *Skrifter*:

1. *Ola Kai Ledang (red.):* Gregorianikk, billedkunst og liturgi i middelalderen.
2. *Dom Eugène Cardine:* Det første året med gregoriansk sang.
3. *Audun Dybdahl:* Matrikkel over sentraleid jordegods i Trøndelag på reformasjonstiden.
4. *Katherine Holman:* Scandinavian Runic Inscriptions in the British Isles: Their Historical Context.
5. *Audun Dybdahl og Jørn Sandnes (red.):* Nordiske middelalderlover. Tekst og kontekst.
6. *Audun Dybdahl (red.):* Middelalderforskningens mangfold. Seminarer ved Senter for middelalderstudier.
7. *Audun Dybdahl Ola Kai Ledang Nils H. Petersen (eds.):* Gregorian Chant and Medieval Music.

Centre for Medieval Studies
Norwegian University of Science and Technology
7034 Trondheim

Senter for middelalderstudier
Norges teknisk-naturvitenskapelige universitet
7034 Trondheim

Tlf.: 73 59 83 49
Fax: 73 59 69 46

Senter for middelalderstudier Skrifter nr. 7

Gregorian Chant and Medieval Music

Proceedings from The Nordic Festival and
Conference of Gregorian Chant
Trondheim, St. Olavs Wake 1997

Audun Dybdahl
Ola Kai Ledang
Nils Holger Petersen (eds.)

TAPIR

© Tapir Publishers and the authors, 1998

ISBN 82-519-1306-3
ISSN 0807-4798

This publication may not be reproduced, stored in a retrieval system or transmitted in any form or by any means; electronic, electrostatic, magnetic tape, mechanical, photo-copying, recording or otherwise, without permission.

Printed by Tapir

NORDIC FESTIVAL AND CONFERENCE OF GREGORIAN CHANT
St. Olavs Wake 1997
TRONDHEIM

We wish to thank the Centre for Medieval Studies, NTNU, for producing an anthology of lectures given at this conference as part of their series of publications.

We would also like to thank the lecturers for being willing to produce shortened versions of their work within the strict time limits of the conference.

We wish to express our thanks to the Centre and to the University of Trondheim for giving financial support to our festival conference.

AMICI CANTUS GREGORIANI NIDROSIAE
(Nidaros Friends of Gregorian Chant)

has since its foundation on November 18th 1984 worked to revive knowledge of Gregorian Chant. This music was sung in our churches from the time when the Christian message was first preached in our land until well into the 18th century, when organs were gradually introduced. Gregorian Chant was for many years a forgotten part of our musical heritage.

Our workshops and seminars have given lay and learned the opportunity to sing according to the traditional notation. In this way we have built up a worldwide network of contacts from California to Japan and Hammerfest to Cameroon.

In spite of a number of simultaneous arrangements in the Gregorian world, 140 enthusiastic participants attended our festival conference.

Our organisation has worked to make the Centre for Medieval Studies a reality. It is therefore a great pleasure for us that the Centre has done us the honour of publishing the conference lectures as part of their series.

Dordi Glærum Skuggevik
Executive Secretary
ACGN

Contents

The Editors' Introduction 9

John Bergsagel:
The Offices and Masses of St. Knud Lavard (d. 1131) 13

Ann-Marie Nilsson:
Links in the Transmission of the *Historia* of St. Erik 29

Eyolf Østrem:
The Early Liturgy of St. Olav 43

Owain Tudor Edwards:
Musical Source Material for a Study of the Medieval Use of Nidaros 59

Ola Kai Ledang:
From *Galdr* to *Paternoster*—
Norse and Christian Music Practices in Snorri's *Heimskringla* 85

Viveca Servatius:
Cantus Sororum—Seven Offices in Honour of the Virgin Mary
Within the Bridgettine Order 107

Eva Rungwald:
Office Antiphons in the First Mode: Context, Structure,
Development and Aesthetics, with Examples of a Working Method   119

Nils Holger Petersen:
Understanding Medieval Chant and Liturgy 139

Nino Albarosa:
Aspekte der menschlichen und wissenschaftlichen Figur
von Dom Eugène Cardine 151

The Editors' Introduction

During the millenium celebrations of the city of Trondheim also a number of different festivals and conferences took place. When the *Amici cantus gregoriani Nidrosiae*, the Trondheim Society for Gregorian Chant, and their dynamic leader Dordi Glærum Skuggevik proposed *Olsok* (Saint Olaf's Day) 1997 as an appropriate occasion for a festival of Gregorian chant, the *Centre for Medieval Studies*, having Gregorian Studies as a central area of its study program, found it natural to support this endeavour. At the time, however, the Centre had not yet appointed its academic staff in this area and was only able to provide financial support for the conference on Gregorian Studies which was planned to take place along with the song festival. The Centre did, however, also express interest in publishing lectures held on this occasion.

For a number of reasons it proved impossible to print all of the contributions which were given orally at the above mentioned conference in Trondheim, July 26–29. We are very content, on the other hand, that so many of the participants were willing to edit their presentations for publication.

The volume we present here reflects both the differences of interest of individual scholars as well as a marked line of division in Gregorian chant scholarship between ecclesiastically oriented, Roman Catholic studies and—at least in principle—non-denominational university approaches to the same materials. It was through the interest in contemporary liturgical matters in the Roman Catholic Church that serious study of the medieval chant manuscripts was started in the 19th century, notably by the monks of Solemnes in France. As it is well known, their scholarship, which in fact led to the re-adoption of the old traditions in Roman Catholic liturgy in 1903, has involved detailed semiological analyses of early notational practices in connection with a historically oriented study of the development of the liturgy and the chant.

It is only natural that the ecclesiastically oriented basis of this research at the same time created certain difficulties. The Counter-Reformation attitudes of the Tridentine Council (held between 1545 and 1563) on liturgical matters were very much a part of the presuppositions of the research in question. Thus, for instance, the large amounts of medieval tropes and sequences (basically suppressed in the tridentine missal and breviary) preserved in manuscripts already from the early tenth century did not enter within the horizon of this scholarship, which has perpetuated the idea of a liturgical decline from an original Roman liturgy and chant in the centuries following the Carolingian reforms. Partly, this attitude can be seen reflected even in university textbooks in the Protestant North!

It would be an illusion to think of the studies of medieval liturgy and chant carried out in (more or less) independent universities mainly in Europe and the USA as representing a valuefree scholarship. Any scholar and any human being is necessarily influenced to some extent by current ideas and prejudices. Even so, the relative independence of most universities and the mere idea of critical scholarship—plus the fact that the medieval liturgy in this context became an object of interest to several disciplines, including musicology, comparative literature, drama, history and art history, and even sociology and anthropology—have made their impact not the least on the questions that have been asked of the historical materials of the medieval liturgy. Certainly, tropes, sequences, and other items later suppressed from the medieval liturgy have been studied seriously by scholars from the United States to Sweden and Finland, and from Italy and Spain to Norway and recently medieval liturgy has even become a subject of interest in modern discourses like *cultural studies* and *interarts studies*.

Conversely, the "independent" university scholars frequently would not have an intimate acquaintance with a liturgical practice close to the medieval daily celebrations of the office as it is, of course, true in a monastic context in spite of the differences between pre-tridentine and post-tridentine rites.

A very different aspect of the study of medieval liturgy and chant has to do with the transmission of the centralized Frankish-Roman chant and the resulting variety in manuscripts from different geographical (and ethnic) areas. Whereas the early modern liturgiology was mainly concerned with the quest for an original form of Roman Catholic worship, modern scholarship has to a large degree given up this idea in favour of the concept of local liturgical uses. Each local liturgical practice can be understood as an original use in its own right. Such a view is also reflected in the national orientation of some parts of modern scholarship. Here the interest is no longer to find the roots of the Roman Catholic or Lutheran (or other forms of Protestant) liturgy but rather to search for national roots at the earliest stages of the reception of the international Latin chant into the country in question.

The aspects mentioned are all represented in the essays of this volume, although not unambiguously so in each individual contribution. Three scholars from the Scandinavian countries, John Bergsagel, Ann-Marie Nilsson, and Eyolf Østrem discuss the three most important Royal saints' offices from Denmark, Sweden, and Norway, giving insight into the formative years of the establishing of a Latin Christian cult in these countries. Owain Tudor Edwards takes up the difficult problem of the (lack of) musical source materials from the medieval Nidaros liturgy, whereas Ola Kai Ledang turns our attention to the Norse context and the information about liturgical chant that can be found in the writings of an author not normally drawn upon in this respect, the famous Icelandic historian Snorri Sturluson who wrote in the early 13th century. Viveca Servatius presents offices for the Virgin Mary from the late-medieval Swedish order of St. Bridget (Birgitta). Eva Rungwald in her presentation concentrates on Office antiphons of the first mode in an attempt to account for developments of this particular liturgical item during an important stage of its long history. Nils Holger Petersen addresses some fundamental questions concerning the modern appropriation of medieval chant. Finally, also a personal tribute to the important Solesmes monk and scholar Dom Eugène Cardine by Nino Albarosa has been included in German (as it was given at the conference).

Since antiquity, the theoretical concept of music, *musica*, belonging to the mathematical curriculum of the seven liberal arts of the higher education, was sharply distinguished from musical practice, although the writings of St. Augustine (354–430) manifest his particular interest in both aspects. It is interesting, however, that during the Carolingian age (the rule of Charlemagne—between 768 and 814—and his sons), when (according to many of the leading scholars in the field today) the so-called Gregorian chant can be said to have come into existence and when music writing took its beginning, serious attempts were made to combine the two aspects (taking up the legacy of St. Augustine). It is appropriate to ponder the following opening statement from one of the important anonymous Carolingian treatises on music (according to the most recent views dating from some time during the second half of the 9th century), the *scolica enchiriadis*. Its point of view is at the same time theological, mathematical, and esthetical, it is theoretically founded, but practically oriented, representing the Carolingian synthesis and balance, as it is also found in the chants which were given their shape in the important liturgical centres of the Kingdom:

M[aster]: What is music?

D[isciple]: The science of regulating properly the movement of sound.

M: But what does it mean to regulate properly the movement of sound?

D: To control melody so that it sounds sweet. But this must be done in full conformance with the rules. It is clear to me that one who misuses the sweetness of this art for worthless purposes, just as one who does not know how to apply the rules of the discipline where it is necessary, does not regulate sound properly. Rather, only someone with a heart full of devotion sings sweetly to the Lord.

M: You are right in thinking that sweet melodies are well-made only when they serve a good purpose and, likewise, that sacred melodies are not used properly if they are performed unpleasantly without theoretical knowledge.[1]

Audun Dybdahl   *Ola Kai Ledang*   *Nils Holger Petersen*

---

1 Quoted from the recent translation by Raymond Erickson in:
Palisca, Claude V. And Erickson, Raymond (eds), *Musica enchiriadis and Scolica enchiriadis* (New Haven, N.Y. 1995), pp. 33–34.
   The original text is found in Schmid, Hans (ed), *Musica et scolica enchiriadis una cum aliquibus tractatulis adiunctis* (München 1981), pp. 60–61:

M. Musica quid est?

D. Bene modulandi scientia.

M. Bene modulari quid est?

D. Melos suavisonum moderari. Sed haec quantum ad artem. Ceterum non bene modulari video, si quis in vanis suavitate artis abutitur, quemadmodum nec ipse, qui, ubi oportet, arte uti non novit, quamvis quilibet devoto tantum corde Domino dulce canit.

M. Recte putas, non nisi bono usu dulcia mela bene fieri, nec rursum sacris melis bene uti, si sine disciplina iniocundius proferantur. Quocirca cum ecclesiasticis canticis haec disciplina vel maxime necessaria sit, ne incuria vel imperitia deturpentur, videamus, quibus rebus opus sit ad bene modulandi facultatem.

The Offices and Masses of
St. Knud Lavard († 1131)

John Bergsagel

Denmark adopted Christianity only a few years before Norway. It was about the year 960 that King Harald Blåtand (i.e., Harald with a miscoloured tooth) raised at Jelling (near Vejle on Jutland) an impressive rune stone for his father, King Gorm, on which he styles himself "that Harald who conquered all Denmark and Norway and made the Danes Christians." With the new religion came a new music, which must have confronted Scandinavians with a radical change of aesthetic values and one wonders how long it took for the refinement of Gregorian chant to win acceptance. The only evidence known to me that tells of an early Scandinavian response to the music of the new church is in the 12-century "Book of Ely", which provides unusual documentation of at least Knud the Great's susceptibility to it. The author of the "Book of Ely" quotes, in English, a song about King Knud "which is still sung in these parts", as he says—that is to say, it was still being sung more than a hundred years after the event, which must have taken place about 1020–30:

> "Merrily sang the monks of Ely
> as King Knud rowed by.
> 'Row close to the shore, lads,
> so that we can hear the monks' song'." [1]

Though the original missionary activity in Denmark and Sweden came from Germany, contacts of trade and conquest across the North Sea in the ninth, tenth and eleventh centuries, and especially the settlement of that part of England called the Danelaw, ensured that in the early years of Christianity the dominant influence on Denmark came from England (as it did also to Norway). The

---

1 Here modernized; original version in *Liber Eliensis*, ed. E. O. Blake, Camden Society, Third Series, Vol. XCII (London 1962), p. 153.

names of missionaries active in Denmark are mostly Anglo-Saxon or Anglo-Danish, and numerous churches in Denmark were dedicated to Anglo-Saxon saints such as Alban, Bede, Berginus, Botulf, Edmund, Egwin, John of Beverly and Oswald.

The close relations which were early established between the Danish and English churches continued even after England ceased to be ruled by Danish kings. Nowhere is this more apparent than in Odense, principal city of the island of Fyn, described already in the 11th century by Adam of Bremen as "a great city". It was here, kneeling before the altar in the church which he had caused to be built to house the relics of St. Oswald, King of Northumbria (d. 642) and St. Alban, *protomartyr anglorum*, that King Knud II (1080–1086), grandnephew of Knud the Great, was murdered on 10 July, 1086. It was on the advice of an English Benedictine, Hubald (who sometime before 1100 became bishop of Odense), that King Erik Ejegod [Evergood] (1095–1103) applied to King William II Rufus to send him twelve monks from Evesham Abbey (where Ailward, a relative of King Knud the Great, had been abbot) to provide a suitable celebration of his brother, the martyred King Knud, at whose grave miracles had already occurred. A Benedictine priory, a daughter house of Evesham, was thus established at Odense, where the monks, in English fashion, also served as the chapter of the cathedral. Egwin, founder of Evesham, is mentioned together with a number of other English saints in the Odense breviaries, just as Knud is remembered in the Evesham calendar[2] on 10 July. A *Passio* written at about this time, presumably by one of the English monks, may have been prepared for use in connection with the services that were instituted to honour King Knud. Within a short time his canonization was confirmed by papal bull of Paschal II and St. Knud, *protomartyr danorum* was translated with great ceremony on 19 April, 1100 or 1101. An eye-witness to this ceremony, one Ælnoth, a clerk (or perhaps monk) from Canterbury who had been 24 years in Denmark, wrote c. 1122 a full Latin *Life,* a work of considerable literary merit—the first such composition in Danish literature.[3]

The martyrdom of St. Knud *rex* thus provided the occasion for the first attempts at the writing of Danish history. It can also be said that the occasion of his canonization and translation is the first that we can be sure must have prompted the creation and writing down of a musical composition in Denmark,

---

2 Oxford, Bodleian Library MS Barlow 41.
3 See M. Cl. Gertz, *Knud den Helliges Martyrhistorie* (Copenhagen 1907); also M. Cl. Gertz, *Vitae Sanctorum Danorum,* Vol. I (Copenhagen 1908) and, in Danish translation, H. Olrik, *Danske Helgeners Levned*, Vol. I (Copenhagen 1893–4).

which until this time had had no obvious reason for enlarging the liturgical repertory brought into the country by the missionaries. Unfortunately, we find ourselves in a position similar to that in which England found itself before the discovery of the Pierpont-Morgan MS:[4] the music of the proper Office of the *protomartyr danorum*, like that of the *protomartyr anglorum*, has been lost. Our situation in Denmark is even more unhappy than the present situation with regard to St. Alban, however, for even though the music of the Office of St. Alban in the 11th-century Pierpont-Morgan MS is written in staffless neumes which cannot be transcribed, the text is very early and cannot be far removed from the original author, whereas we have no early MS source for St. Knud the King.

The liturgical services composed by the monks at Odense to the honour of King Knud were naturally designed to serve monastic purposes, but in their original form they have all disappeared together with the music to which they were sung. The earliest sources remaining to us of the Offices of St. Knud *rex* are the non-monastic revisions that were printed (without music of course) in the *Breviarum Othiniense* in 1482–3 and again in 1497. Versions also occur in the printed breviaries for Aarhus (1519), Lund (1517) and Roskilde (1517), and Masses are found in the missals printed for Slesvig (1486), Lund (1514) and Copenhagen (= Roskilde) (1519), but no copy of the original monastic Office of the first Danish saint has yet been found.

Until the last century, this was also the situation with regard to the second Danish saint, Duke Knud (best known by his English-derived title "Lavard"). However, about 1825 Baron Carl von Richthofen zu Leszcyn in Oberschlesien bought a manuscript at auction in Leipzig, a codex in quarto size consisting of 66 folios, apparently written by a single hand, presumably in the latter part of the 13th century. The manuscript was found to contain, on the first 49 folios, the proper Offices and Masses, complete with music, for the two feast days of St. Knud Lavard, *In passione* (7 January) and *In translatione* (25 June). These are followed, without a break, by a copy (lacking the last page) of the *Roskilde Chronicle* (ca. 1139–43), which records the early history of Denmark, including the events relating to Knud Lavard, and finally there is a brief but charming parable of a monk who is lured away from his monastery by the irresistibly beautiful song of a bird and finds when he returns that 200 years have passed.

---

4   See J. Bergsagel, "Anglo-Scandinavian Musical Relations Before 1700", *International Musicological Society. Report of the Eleventh Congress, Copenhagen 1972*, (Copenhagen 1974), Vol. I, 263–71; also K. D. Hartzell, "A St. Albans Miscellany in New York", *Mittellateinisches Jahrbuch*, 10. Jahrg. (1975), 20–61.

Appropriately, having regard to its importance as a document relevant to the history of Slesvig-Holstein, this precious manuscript was bequeathed at Baron von Richthofen's death in 1874 to the university library at Kiel, where it now carries the manuscript number S.H. 8 A. 8°.

Knud Lavard was born on St. Gregory's day, 12th March, probably in 1096, the son of King Erik Ejegod and Queen Bodil. King Erik was a brother of St Knud the King, who is said to have insisted in a vision that his nephew be named after him. In 1115 he was given a dukedom in the south of Jutland with responsibility for defending Denmark's southern borders and establishing peace and stability in the borderlands. This he achieved with great success and he won fame and respect for his energetic leadership and stern justice. In 1129 he was given the title of "knés" (that is, lord) over the Obotrits in the western Wendish lands. His growing power began now to worry King Niels (1104–34), and the increasing favour with which he was regarded by the people was viewed with envy by his cousin, Magnus, who saw in Knud Lavard a dangerous rival for his own election to kingship after his father's, Niels's, death. At the king's great Christmas feast in Roskilde in 1130, therefore, Magnus made an appointment with Knud to meet him in Haraldsted Woods, near Ringsted, when the Christmas celebrations were over on the pretext of wanting to discuss some personal matters with his "best friend"; Knud had in fact promised Magnus' mother before she died that he would always be like a good older brother to her son.

On 7th January 1131, the day after the feast of Epiphany had concluded the Christmas season, in spite of several warnings that Magnus was not to be trusted, the good-hearted and loyal Knud set out unarmed for the appointed meeting place. Here he was ambushed and killed by Magnus, together with another cousin, Henrik Skadelaar, and two other conspirators, both named Haakon. At the place where he fell, a well began to flow at which many wonders are reported to have occurred. A pilgrims' chapel was accordingly built, the ruins of which were discovered at the end of the 19th century.

Very soon after the event, about 1137, a *Vita*, a life of Knud Lavard in which he is treated as if he were already a saint, was written by an English Benedictine monk, Robert of Ely. He presumably belonged to the nearby Ringsted Monastery, in whose church Knud Lavard had been buried, and the brothers there began at this time to keep a record of the miracles that occurred at his grave. A wish to have him declared a saint was soon expressed, but it was not until 1169 that permission was granted, when the application sponsored by his son, King Valdemar the Great (1157–82) resulted in a letter being sent from Pope Alexander III, dated at Benevent, 8 November, 1169, in which he declared that, since "Knud, of blessed memory, ... while he lived was distinguished by an honourable and praiseworthy life in accordance with Christian virtues, and that after his death a well gushed forth, a blind man regained his sight and the almighty and merciful God was moved by him to perform many other wonderful works . . . . We have now . . . . on the advice of Our brothers decided to enter his name in the list of saints . . . . ".[5] The date appointed for his Translation was 25 June, 1170, and on this day, with great pomp and ceremony and in the presence of a great assembly, his earthly remains were placed on the altar of St. Maria's—now St. Bendt's (i.e., Benedict's)—monastery church in Ringsted.

The celebration of a new saint naturally required a proper Office—that is, text and music appropriate to the various services of the new saint's feast days—and it appears that that which was "composed" for St. Knud Lavard has by great good fortune been preserved in the manuscript now kept in the university library in Kiel. Though it is certainly a late 13th-century manuscript (because of its liturgical content usually referred to as an *Ordinal*), it is equally certain that it is not itself a liturgical book—the presence of the *Roskilde Chronicle* is proof of that—but rather a library copy of an earlier liturgical source. That earlier source, it is reasonable to suppose, must have been prepared—"composed"—in a period of intense activity in the first months of the year 1170, in the period between the reception of Pope Alexander's letter, which is dated at Benevent, 8 November 1169, and the actual Translation ceremony, which took place in Ringsted on 25 June, 1170. This suggestion of concentrated work is supported by the stylistic consistency to be observed throughout the work; it is surely one man's work—or more probably, one man has composed the entire text and another has composed or adapted all the music. One notices too that, although Knud Lavard is referred to in the text as a saint, and that the date appointed by Pope Alexander for the Translation is stated, the events of the Translation in the presence of the king, the archbishops of Lund and Uppsala, the bishop of Oslo, the eight Danish bishops (no doubt including Bishop Absalon of Roskilde) and all the other high dignitaries are not mentioned, no doubt because they had not yet taken place.

Furthermore, though the manuscript was found in Germany, there is no reason to suppose that it originated there. Knud Lavard was celebrated all over Denmark throughout the middle ages and various versions of his Office are found—though without music—in the printed liturgical books that were issued for the cathedrals of Roskilde, Aarhus, Slesvig and Lund, for example, shortly

---

5   See "Pave Alexander III's kanonisationsbulle" in *Catholica* XXVII (1970), 70–72.

before the Reformation rendered them useless. The manuscript now in Kiel, however, is the only source containing the entire Office with music and there is an important difference between the way it is transmitted there as compared to all the other sources: in the Kiel manuscript it occurs in a form that is intended for use in a monastery. This can be seen most clearly in the fact that there are 12 Lessons at Matins, where an ordinary (secular) cathedral would only read 9, even on a feast day of high rank. For each of the feast days there are thus 8 historical Lessons (in the two first Nocturnes) and 4 Homilies (in the third Nocturne) and the 16 historical Lessons together provide a biography of considerable historical value, the careful treatment and attention to detail of which distinguish it from the usual saint's Office. In addition, the Responses, proper Antiphons, Hymns and Sequences add a parallel versified historical account (those of the Responses are referred to internally as an "Historia"), instead of providing evidence of his saintliness by telling of the miracles associated with him, as one would normally expect. That the monastery where it originated has belonged to the Order of the Black Monks, that is, the Order of St. Benedict, is indicated by, among other things, the hymn *Te decet laus* at the close of Matins, as is obligatory in Benedictine practice. It can scarcely be supposed that the Office of St. Knud Lavard in all its completeness—it represents a complete cycle of the Office Hours and Mass that were held in a monastery in the course of a day, every third hour on average, on each of the two days that were assigned to him in the church calendar—can have originated anywhere else than at Ringsted Monastery, in whose church the murdered Duke Knud was buried in 1131, where various miracles were observed at his grave and recorded and where his earthly remains were translated in 1170. The Kiel manuscript is accordingly now usually referred to as the Ringsted Ordinal.

In the absence of the original monastic Office of St. Knud the King and its music, we can risk the claim, I think, that the Office of St. Knud Lavard, as transmitted in the Ringsted Ordinal, is the oldest surviving contribution to the liturgical repertoire of the church that has originated in Denmark. However I would hesitate to claim that it is a Danish contribution—that is, made by Danes. It is a composition of distinguished quality and the church, one must remember, was still young in the northern countries at that time. Philologists have been inclined to attribute the honour of having written the texts of the Offices to one of the English monks that, as is well known, were brought to Denmark by the Danish kings, and I am inclined to agree with this opinion as regards the music as well.

Indeed, the composers of the Offices have left a number of traces of their debt to the practice of the English church. It is too complicated a subject to attempt to deal with thoroughly under the present circumstances, but I can perhaps illustrate this interesting and valuable evidence of cultural influence with some examples from the first Offices in the manuscript, 1st Vespers and Matins:

On the first folio of the manuscript, at the beginning of the Office of Vespers of the Feast *In passione* (i.e., 7 January), where one expects four antiphons with their respective psalms, there is written only the intonation of the antiphon *Tecum principium*. (Pl. 1) It was obviously expected that it would be understood from this that the antiphons and psalms to be sung here would be those sung at Vespers on the Feast of Epiphany, 6 January (which, of course, coincides with first Vespers on the eve of St. Knud Lavard's day), as they are prescribed in the liturgy of the English church. (Ill. 1) It is difficult to understand it otherwise, since in the Roman tradition *Tecum principium* does not occur at Epiphany but at Christmas.

Furthermore, the melodies of the Hymns *Gaudet mater ecclesia* (at Vespers) and *Primo proscriptos patria* (at Matins) have in all likelihood been introduced from England. The poems of the two hymns appear to be new, more or less freely composed, but the music has proven to be adapted in both cases and the tune of *Gaudet mater ecclesia,* especially, (Pl. 2) presents us with an interesting performance problem. The melody of *Gaudet mater ecclesia* (Ex. 1) was thought at one time to be original to this text and Angul Hammerich was even persuaded that it had a particularly Nordic character.[6] However, in 1935 Handschin pointed out that it was yet another occurrence of the melody that Peter Wagner had recognized as a voice-exchange melody (for example, with the text *Jam lucis orto sidere* in the Nivers MS, Paris, B.N. n.acq. 1235),[7] which in two English sources (the York MS, Cambridge, St.Johns 102 and the Durham [Coldingham] Breviary, London, Br. Lib. Harleian MS 4664) is actually written out, here with the text *Nunc sancte nobis,* as two-part harmony in score.[8] (Pl. 3) This led him to suggest that this hymn may be the earliest example of polyphony in a Danish source.

Curiously, the second verse of *Gaudet mater ecclesia*, beginning *Frustrata legis federe*, is provided in the MS with another melody and it too is borrowed. Stäblein concluded that it was an English tune[9]—at least the earliest source known to him was the Worcester Antiphonal, where it has the text *Ad ce-*

---

6   A. Hammerich, *Mediæval Musical Relics of Denmark* (Leipzig 1912), 82.
7   P. Wagner, "Ein versteckter Diskantus" in *Festschrift für Johannes Wolf* (Berlin 1929), 207.
8   J. Handschin, "Die älteste Dokument für die Pflege der Mehrstimmigkeit in Dänemark", *Acta Musicologica* VII (1935), 67.
9   B. Stäblein, *Monumenta monodica medii aevi* I: *Hymnen* (Kassel 1956), 562.

nam agni providi,[10] though incipits indicate that it could also be used for *Nunc sancte nobis* and it is still used with the text *Jesu corona virginum*. Both Handschin and Stäblein failed, however, to observe that this melody too can be sung polyphonically as a rondellus.[11] (Ex. 2) Whether it—or either of them—was sung in this way in Denmark, and if so, whether the two tunes were alternatives or were sung to alternate verses, is impossible to prove. It is also tempting to consider a performance which adopts the metrical rhythm of the poetic text. (Ex. 3)

The melody of the second hymn, *Primo proscriptos*, sung at Matins, (Ill. 2) was also assumed to be a Danish composition, since it was apparently not known elsewhere, until I found it with the familiar text *Jam lucis orto sidere* in the MS London, Sion College, Arc. L 40. 2. L. 1—again a MS of York Use.[12] (Ex. 4)

One observes also that the gospel reading in the third Nocturne (Ill. 3), which here is taken from John chap. XII, is the reading prescribed for a martyr in the English liturgy, whereas the Roman tradition prefers a reading from the Gospel according to Luke.

The Response at the end of the last (12th) Lesson is provided with an extended treatment which is rather sophisticated, confidently and very successfully carried out by a practiced hand. Here we find that instead of the *Te Deum*, with which Matins should normally end, the Response *Decus regni et libertas* is repeated and troped with a *Prosa: Qui conducis servos crucis*, an extended poem sung to melodic phrases taken from one of the Response's *neumas*, after which there is a return to the Response at the point where it was interrupted in order to sing the last couple of words. (Ex. 5) Responses with *Prosas* are comparatively rare in monastic manuscripts and it serves here to emphasize the dignity and festive character of the occasion.

The Offices and Masses of St. Knud Lavard are filled with details of musical, liturgical and historical interest, not least of which are the numerous points of relationship they reveal to the Offices of other Scandinavian, and especially Anglo-Saxon, royal martyrs. As a document from the first 200 years of the church's existence in Denmark, it can tell us a great deal about the missionary period in Scandinavia. It is of course too rich a material for so short a presentation, but I am preparing a complete edition which I hope will represent it more satisfactorily in the not too distant future.

---

10 *Paléographie musicale* XII (Paris 1922–23), 7+
11 J. Bergsagel, "Liturgical Relations between England and Scandinavia: as seen in selected musical fragments from the 12th and 13th centuries", in *Föredrag och Diskussionsinlägg från Nordiskt Kollokvium III i Latinsk Liturgiforskning* (Helsingfors 1975), 17.
12 J. Bergsagel, "Songs for St. Knud the King", *Musik & Forskning* 6 (1980), 152.

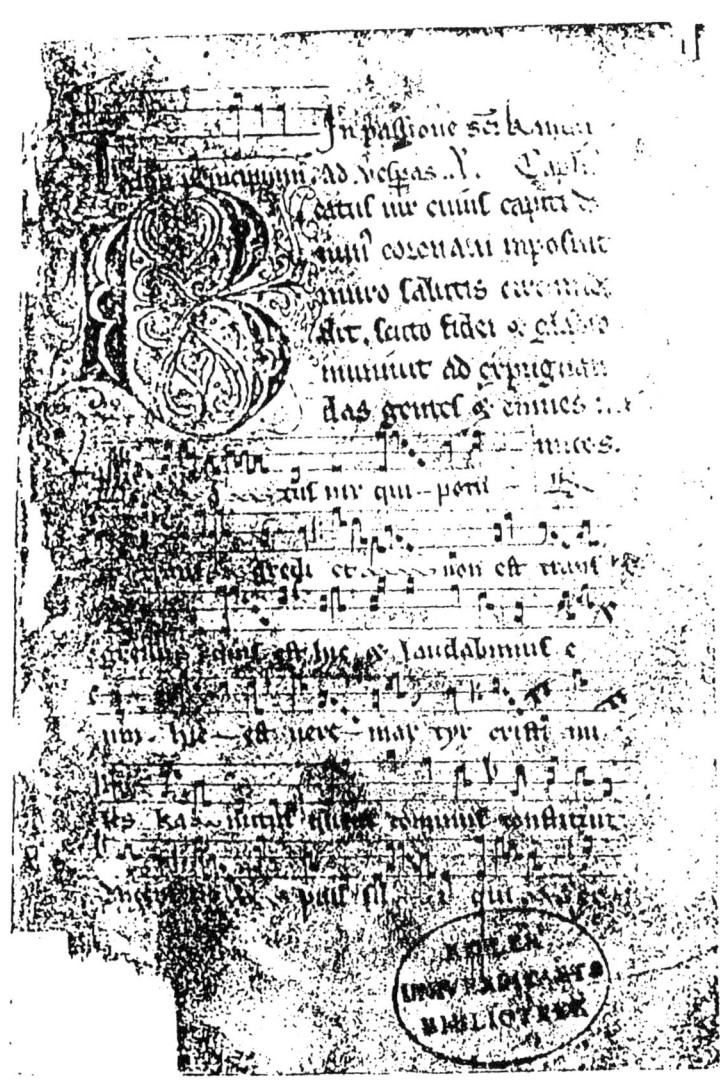

Pl. 1: *In passione sancti Kanuti. Ad vesperas* (Kiel UB MS S.H. 8.A.8°, f. 1)

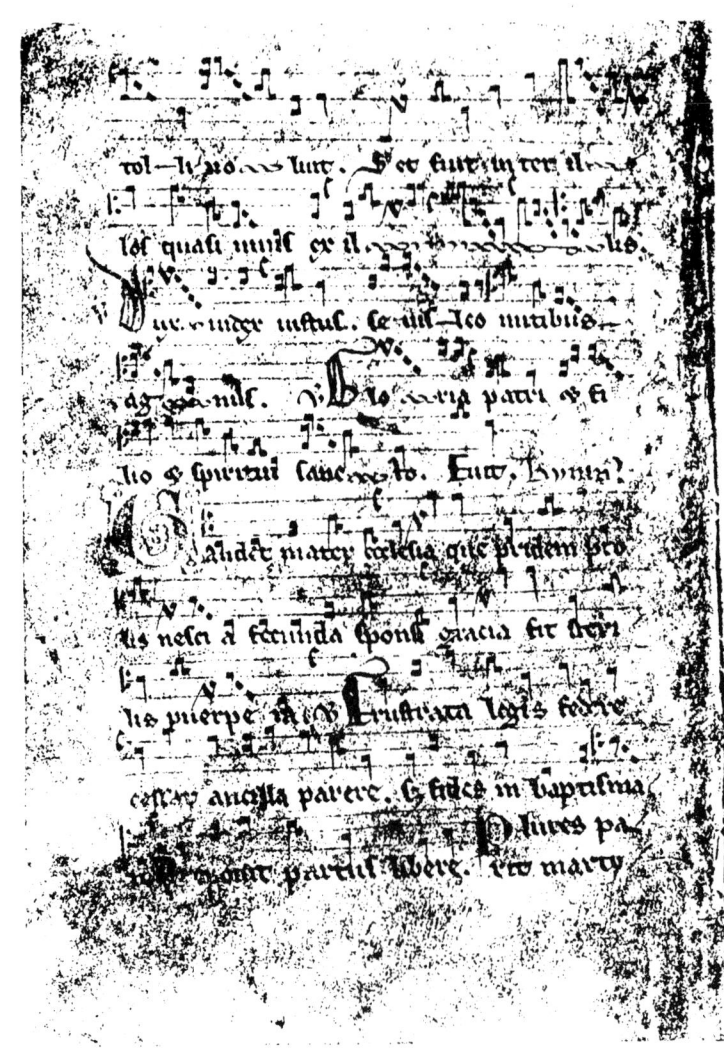

Pl. 2: *In passione sancti Kanuti. Ad vesperas* (Kiel UB MS S.H. 8.A.8°, f. 1v)
Hymnus: Gaudet mater ecclesia, V. Frustrata legis federe

Pl. 3: *Nunc sancte nobis (= Gaudet mater ecclesia)* as rondellus in score
(London, Br.Lib. Harl. MS 4664, f. 182v)

Ex. 1: Hymn *Gaudet mater ecclesia*, also as rondellus

* Notes a - f - g here in Worcester MS are preferable and result in better discant

Ex. 2: Hymn, v. 2 *Frustrata legis federe,* also as rondellus

Ex. 3: Hymn *Gaudet mater ecclesia*, as metrical rondellus

Ex. 4: Hymn *Primo proscriptos* and (lower notes and slurs) *Jam lucis orto sidere* in Sion Coll., Arc.L.40.2.L.1

Ex. 5: Final melisma of *R. Decus regni*, with Prosa trope *Qui conducis*

In passione sancti Kanuti
Ad [primas] Vesperas

V[ersiculus]. Deus, in adjutorium meum intende.
R[esponsio]. Domine, ad adjuvandum me festina.
Gloria Patri
Alleluia.

Antiphona super psalmos: Tecum principium in die virtutis tuae ...
    Ps. 109: Dixit Dominus Domino meo ...
A. Redemptionem misit Dominus populo suo
    Ps. 110: Confitebor tibi Domine in toto corde meo
A. Exortum est in tenebris lumen rectis corde
    Ps. 111: Beatus vir qui timet Dominum
A. De fructu ventris tui
    Ps. 131: Memento Domine David
Capitulum: Beatus vir, cujus capiti Dominus coronam inposuit
R[esponsorium] Beatus vir qui potuit transgredi et non est transgressus
    V[ersus] Dux judex justus sevis leo
    V. Gloria Patri
Hymnus: Gaudet mater ecclesia
V. Ora pro nobis, beate Kanute.
R. Ut digni efficiamur promissionibus Christi.
A. *ad Magnificat* Ave martyr, dux Danorum, ave decus Dacie
    Canticum: Magnificat anima mea
Collecta: Deus, in cujus fide gloriosus dux Kanute firmiter incedens,
V. Benedicamus Domino.
R. Deo gratias.

Ill. 1: Office of St. Knud Lavard *In passione,* First Vespers

Ad matutinum

V. Deus, in adjutorium meum intende.
R. Domine, ad adjuvandum me festina.
Gloria Patri
Alleluia.
(3 times) V. Domine, labia mea aperies.
    R. Et os meum annuntiabit laudem tuam.
Ps. 3: Domine, quid multiplicati sunt qui tribulant me?
Invitatorium: Veni turba fidelium, Dei adora filium,
    Ps. 94: Venite, exultemus Domino, jubilemus Deo salutari nostro
Hymnus: Primo proscriptos patria

Ill. 2: Office of St. Knud Lavard *In passione,* beginning of Matins

[IN III. NOCTURNO] *Ad cantica*

A. Dux Kanute, da ducatum,
  Canticum: (Eccl. XIV, 22, XV, 3-4,6) Beatus vir, qui in sapientia
  Canticum: (Jer. XVII, 7-8) Benedictus vir, qui confidit in Domino
  Canticum: (Eccl. XXXI, 8-31) Beatus vir, qui inventus est
V. Justus ut palma florebit.
R. Sicut cedrus Libani multiplicabitur.
Pater noster
Absolution
Lector: Jube Domne benedicere
Benedictio
Lectio sancti evangelii secundum Johannem (XII, 24 sqq.): In illis. Dixit Jhesus discipulis suis: Amen, amen dico vobis nisi granum frumenti cadens in terra mortuum fuerit, ipsum solum manet. Et reliqua.
[*Lectio ix.*] Omelia lectionis ejusdem. Ostendit nobis rerum universarum
V. Tu autem ... R. Deo gratias.
R. In viis suis omnibus
  V. De carnis ergastulo fidelis anima
...
Lectio xii. Si granum mortuum fuerit
V. Tu autem ... R. Deo gratias.
R. Decus regni et libertas
  V. Cetibus angelicis junctus
  V. Gloria Patri
R. Decus regni
  Prosa: Qui conducis servos crucis crucifixi numine
V. Dominus vobiscum. R. Et cum spiritu tuo.
Sequentia sancti evangelii secundum Johannem (XII, 24-26): In illis. Dixit Jesus discipulis suis...
Hymnus: Te decet laus, te decet hymnus
Kyrie
Pater noster
Collecta: Deus, qui sanctam nobis hujus diei sollempnitatem in honore beati Kanuti martyris tui consecrasti, adesto familie tue precibus, et da, ut cujus hodie festa celebramus in terris, ejus meritis et intercessionibus adjuventur in celis. Per Dominum nostram.
V. Dominus vobiscum. R. Et cum spiritu tuo.
V. Benedicamus Domino ... R. Deo gratias.

Ill. 3: Office of St. Knud Lavard *In passione,* Matins, beginning and end of Nocturne III

Links in the Transmission of the *Historia* of St. Erik

Ann-Marie Nilsson

Erik Jedvardsson seems to have become king of at least part of present-day Sweden in 1156. The 'Kings' chronicle' (Konungakrönikan), dated c. 1250, in the Early West Gothic Law *(Äldre Västgötalagen)* mentions Erik as the twelfth Christian king in Sweden, victim of a murder and working miracles as a saint. The remaining information about him—all based upon oral tradition, as it seems—is given in the legend that tells *inter alia* about a military expedition to Finland and his murder by a Danish pretender to the throne on Ascension Day 1160.

After his death, people began telling about miracles associated with him, and he acquired the status of a holy king and martyr, though he was never canonised by the pope; this possibly took place with the support of an archbishop.

St. Erik's life, death, enshrinement (in Old Uppsala, probably in 1167, or between 1167 and 1196), his relics, when and how they were moved (translated) to the new cathedral in present-day Uppsala (according to diocesan tradition, on January 24, 1273)—these problems are among those most intensely discussed within medieval Swedish history. His local cult and liturgy, with a *historia,* containing chants used especially for his day, spread from Uppsala to other Swedish dioceses and some Danish dioceses. By the early 15th century he had come to rank as a national saint, and, together with Olaf and Cnut, as one of the three saintly kings of the North.[1]

An edition of the *historia* for St. Erik is presently being prepared in co-operation with HISTORIAE, a series of editions of offices inaugurated by the study group *Cantus planus* of the International Musicological Society.[2]

---

1 Thordeman 1954. Booklet Musica Sveciae MSCD 103, "The historia of St. Erik".
2 For information about this group, see Hiley 1993, p. 855–858.

The *Historia* and its History

There are many links in this liturgical tradition of more than 300 years. In *written tradition,* at least 43 notated sources are preserved (8 codices, 35 fragments). Five of them contain a complete office. For the CD-recording of the original short form of the office (made mainly by singers from the Schola Hungarica and the Malmö Conservatory), three fragments were used—early representative links in the transmission of the chants.

"Tradition" might, however, be conceived as embracing something more than what we find in written sources. It certainly comprises variants. There is also the oral tradition, as well as its context: the general availability of melodies and melodic formulas from which this very *historia* has evolved. Even referential systems of individuals transmitting the tradition by rote-learning might be regarded as links in the tradition.

The *historia* for St. Erik indicates that an "opus" concept is quite foreign to some medieval plainchant. The chants for St. Erik were not created all at once. Toivo Haapanen, in his pioneering work from 1927, stated that chants were incorporated into the office in three stages, and the inclusion of several more sources in my investigation has provided support for his conclusions:

First the Gospel antiphons in trochaic meter, belonging to the oldest *stratum* of the *historia,* showing British influence and dating perhaps from the mid-13th century;

second, in early 14th-century sources we find a complete office in a widespread, short form with one nocturn, where Dominican influence is evident. This short form with psalm antiphons and responsories, written in Leonine hexameters, and hymn was used until the end of the Middle Ages—in some dioceses presumably as the only form. It may have been written in connection with a second cult wave after the mid-13th century (c. 1270–1290?)[3]. Other chants for Erik's Day, presumably dating from the same period, are the sequence and the Alleluia verse for Mass; possibly also the Gospel antiphon for Lauds *Corona fulgens*. Here, I will deal with a few office chants from this original version.

It is well known that before any *historia* with its chants was complete, the appropriate psalms were given. A proper legend was written and used for recitation in Matins, and collections of miracle stories could be used as a source for chant texts. The melodic material for the chants could consist of

---

3 A few sources from the 14th century use only one psalm antiphon—*antiphona sola*—for 1st Vespers.

- simply a melodic *style,* or
- antiphon *types,* and *formulas* for responsory verses, or even
- extant *melodies* to be adapted to new texts.

There is one case of strict borrowing "sub notis" from the office for St. Dominic in the St. Erik historia, namely the antiphon *Correxit.* The 1st antiphon for Lauds *Hostia grata,* on the other hand, is partly adapted.

The hymn melody is somewhat special: the last of its four lines is identical to the ending of the hymn melody for St. Dominic.[4] There are many formulas that are heard in the offices for St. Dominicus and St. Peter the martyr.

Third "layer": In some dioceses, two nocturns were added, resulting in a late, extended form with three nocturns. Domestic influence is apparent in the use of melodies from the later historia for St. Eskil for the new texts.

Of these nocturns, in Linköping and Uppsala respectively, there are two different "versions" or redactions (Haapanen 1927). Of the still extant notated sources, three[5] have the "Uppsala version" and one[6] the "Linköping version" (which means that the extended form is late and quite rare).

The reason why St. Erik's Day was celebrated for such a long time with only one nocturn is that it fell on May 18, i.e. during the Easter period when one nocturn was the rule in Sweden—even for the veneration of important saints.

Once or twice a century, however, St. Erik's Day falls outside the movable period of Easter, when three nocturns were the norm for a solemn feast day. Also the celebration of Erik's *translatio* (the removal of his remains) in Uppsala on 24 January called for three nocturns. Both these circumstances may explain the appearance of two more nocturns with new chants in the *historia* of St. Erik about 1400, as is reflected in some of the 15th and early 16th century sources mentioned above.

A few late sources—codices and fragmentary sources for which an Uppsala provenance cannot be ruled out—contain two Gospel antiphons for the week ("infra octavam" or "per hebdomadam"): *Magnificemus dominum* and *Benedictus es domine,* written in a kind of iambic dimeter (like the hymns). Haapanen did not mention them in the article referred to here, but I feel that they may be part of the *translatio* office celebrated in Uppsala. Lundén (1960) put forward the hypothesis that they belong to the same second stage as the short form of the office.

---

4   M 247 a in Moberg & Nilsson 1991; see also Nilsson 1990.
5   Skara musikhandskrift nr. 1, KB A 96, RA ANT 161. The Uppsala version is in the *AH.*
6   ÅLA Gummerus I:5.

No author or composer of the chants is known. Haapanen found it likely that the creators might be found in the Dominican convent of Sigtuna. Israel Erlandsson's name has been mentioned in connection with the *vita,* but has not seriously been proposed. For the two extra nocturns, Nicolaus Hermanni, the bishop in Linköping 1374–1391, has been suggested as a possible author.

The Legend

The contents of the lessons recited for Matins also differ very much between sources or groups of sources, as might be expected in any medieval office. Most text versions seem to be based on, or excerped from, what is usually considered *a complete text,* the so-called "standard version" of the legend. E.g. the printed breviary for Nidaros (Trondheim) contains only the beginning of the "standard legend". Some other printed breviaries have abridged versions of the "standard legend". Most sources examined have their own individual selections from and subdivisions of the legend for the lessons.

The legend has usually been assumed to be contemporary with the office (i.e. not earlier than c. 1270). The existence of an older and more expansive form, maybe as early as the end of 12th century, has been discussed. There are no traces of such a version in any source, except that the "standard" legend says *"reliqua vite eius et translacio sancti corporis ac miracula . […] que hic omissa sunt breuitatis causa . alibi scripta sunt"* (other facts about his life and the *translatio* of his holy body, that has here been omitted to keep this text short, are written elsewhere). That passage is found in six manuscripts only, of which the earliest one is the Registrum Upsaliense (1344).

I would suggest another hypothesis: this legend is a puzzle. Since the phrases—or "elements", to use a suitable term advanced by the *Corpus Troporum*—of the legend were apparently selected at will, and if this was a common way of constructing the lessons, the "element" quoted above may have been formulated in order to be incorporated with extant readings, in case other elements of the legend were left out *brevitatis causa.* See Table.

Sources …

My proposed edition will, in accordance with the editions within the HISTORIAE series, concentrate on one point of the tradition and contain a version from a selected main source. Having to select my main source for the edition, I chose a late 15th century codex in Turku, Finland that stands out as a good representative for a stable tradition: Gummerus I:3 gives a version similar to several other sources.[7]

However, as many sources as possible have been studied, in order to

1) make certain that the main source is a representative one, and

2) form the basis for a commentary.

Such a comparative study might result in a *stemma,* a model of relationships. Usually such a model is expected to show the existence of an original version from which later versions emanate, and increasing differences between versions in the course of time. But comparisons of versions of Nordic medieval chants often show exactly the opposite: early preserved sources differ more in details, while the later ones seem to have agreed upon more similar versions.

---

[7] Sources preserved in Finland and with probable Finnish provenance use to have traits in common, both in notational details and disposition of the content of the legend. Most of the sources that use only one antiphon for first Vespers belong to this group.

Table. (See next page). Disposition of parts of the so-called "standard legend" text in selected sources

Text incipits of passages from the "standard legend" (in the Codex Vat. reg. lat. 525) are given in the first column. Lectio I–IX in Roman numerals.

None of the sources examined has exactly the same disposition of elements as anyone else, except a group of fragmentary sources. Although some passages are missing in some early fragments (RA BR 263, BR 265 and BR 420, not represented in the Table), these seem to have the identical disposition as HUB br 68.

When there are three lessons, these are presumably intended for the saint's day. However, if nine lessons were to be read, the last six (or last three) readings may have been drawn from the *commune sanctorum* (cf. C 435 and the printed Danish breviaries). In manuscript C 416 the text is divided into three lessons and subdivided (here: a–b–c) into nine.

The six lessons from the vita in the printed breviaries *Breviarium Lundense* and *Breviarium Roscildense* are identical. (Also the *Breviarium Lincopense* contains six readings from the vita with abbreviated text versions.) All printed breviaries have shorter versions than that for Uppsala diocese, esp. the *Breviarium Strengnense,* that stops at "Cum … 3:am".

(x)   = missing in a fragmentary source, either due to damage, or never represented.
var.   = variant reading
abbr.   = abbreviated version
o   = not present in the source

Standard legend VAT525, Reg.Ups. early 15th c., 1344	BrUpsal. print. 1496	KB A 99 Ups. S 15	C 416 c. 1380	BrAros print. 1513	Br.Roscild.*) print. 1517	Br Nidaros print. 1519
Gloriosi	I	I	I a	I	I abbr.	I abbr.
Exstitit	I	I	I a	I	I abbr.	I
Hic regno	I	I	I a	I	I abbr.	I
In regali	I	I	I a	II	II abbr.	II
Imitatus namque	II	II	I b	II	o	II
Primo ad	II	II	I b	II	III abbr.	II
deinde ad	II	II	I b	II	o	II abbr.
Nam upsal.	II	II	I c	II	o	III
Primo &	II	II	I c	II	o	III
deinde re.	II	II	I c	II	o	III
Sicque pacem	III	III	I c	II	o	o
Cum - 3:am	III	III	I c	III	o	o
O principem	III	III	I c	o	o	o
Verum quia	IV	IV	II a	o	o	o
ideo sanctus	IV	IV	II a	o	IV var.	o
Qualiter	V	IV	II b	o	o	o
propter ieiun.	V	IV	II b	o	o	o
Postremo ..	V	V	II b	o	o	o
coadunato	V	V	II b	o	IV var.	o
ipsosque	V	V	II b	o	IV var.	o
Cumque tan.	VI	V	II c	o	V abbr.	o
interrogatus	VI	V	II c	o	V abbr.	o
Imitatus in h.	VI	VI	II c	o	o	o
Convocato	VII	VI	II c	o	o	o
Currente	VII	VII	III a	o	VI abbr.	o
Magnum ...	VII	VII	III a	o	o	o
ex hereditate	VII	VII	III a	o	o	o
Unde et q.	VIII	VII	III a	o	VI abbr.	o
Instabat die	VIII	VII	III a	o	VI abbr.	o
Cumque illa	IX	VIII	III b	o	o	o
Sinite me ...	IX	VIII	III b	o	o	o
Quos illi belli	IX	IX	III b	o	o	o
Sicque (i.) de	o	IX	III c	o	(VI var.?)	o
Hoc autem	o	IX	III c	o	o	o
Recedentib.	o	IX	III c	o	o	o
Erat ibidem	o	IX	III c	o	o	o
Reliqua	o	o	o	o	o	o
Que hic	o	o	o	o	o	o
Passus est	o	IX	III var.	III	o	o
Regnante ihu	o	o	III c	III	o	o
(Feast:)	Translatio	Translatio		In die	In die	In die
					BrLund.=Rosc.	

HUB br 68 & al.	C 507	KB A 50	LEO 65	C 435	KB A 56	C 84	C 463	BR s.n.
14th & 15th c.	15th c.	1485	14/15th c.	late 15th c.	early 15th c.	c. 1500	14/15th c.	15th c.
(I)	I	I	I	I	I	I	I	I
I	I	I	I	I	I	o	I	I
I	II	I	I	I	I	[I]	I	I
I	II	I	I	II	I	I	II	I
(I)	III	II	II	o	I	o	II	I
I	III	II	II	o	I	I	II	I
I	III	II	II	o	I	I	II	I
II	III	II	II	II	I	o	II	I
II	III	II	II	II var.	I	o	II	I
II	IV	III	II	II	I	[I]	II	I
II	IV	III	II	o	II	II var.	o	I
III	V	III	III	o	II	o	o	I
III	V	o	III	o	II	III var.	o	I
(III)	VI	IV	IV	o	o	o	o	II
III	VII	IV	IV	o	o	III var.	o	II
o	VIII	IV	V	o	o	o	o	II
o	VIII	IV	V	o	o	III var.	o	II
o	IX	V	V	III	II	III var.	o	o
o	IX	V	V	III		o	o	o
o	IX	V	(x)	III	II	o	o	o
o		V	(x)	IV	II abbr.	o	o	o
o		V	(x)	IV	II	o	o	o
o		V	(x)	o	o	o	o	o
o		VI	(x)	o	II	III var.	o	o
o		VII	(x)	V	III	III var.	o	III
o		VII	(x)	V	III	III	o	III
o		VII	(x)	V	III	III var.	o	III
o		VII	(x)	VI	III	III var.	o	III
o		VII	(x)	VI	III	III var.	o	III
o		VIII	(x)	o	III	o	o	III
o		VIII	(x)	o	III	o	o	III
o		VIII	(x)	o	III	III var.	o	III
o		IX	(x)	o	III	o	o	III
o		IX	(x)	o	III	o	III	III
o		IX	(x)	o	o	o	III	III
o		IX	(x)	o	III var.	o	III	III
o		IX	(x)	o	III var.	o	o	III
o		IX	(x)	o	III var.	o	o	III
o		IX	(x)	o	III	o	III	III
o		IX	(x)	o	III	o	III	III
[In die]	Translatio	utroque tot.dupl.			Aboense			

... and Variation

Our psychology teacher at upper-secondary school, Hjalmar Sundén, used to emphasize the importance of the psychology of perception. Therefore, I was pleased to see that a musicologist, Leo Treitler, had applied this to aurally transmitted music. Among other fundamental things, Treitler states:[8]

> "Perceiving is not passive reception, it is active organizing. [...] Remembering (re-organizing) depends on perception. [...] We strive to assimilate newly presented material into the setting of patterns. [...] In perceiving we draw out certain salient features of the matter presented, that are for us especially prominent. They serve as signposts for the process of assimilating and reorganizing, and play a central role in remembering ... which is an active process of grouping appropriate details about such salient features. [...] Beginnings and ends provide focal points of the reconstruction. [...] Form—as well as salient detail—is persistent and is therefore an important factor." (First comes the whole, then details.)

To exemplify such results of an oral tradition, I will provide an illustration. An early source, the fragment A 103 k 139/ANT 26 (dated c. 1300?)[9] might stand as an example of melodies written down from memory and transformed in the process of reconstruction and reorganization. It is a fragment, a double folio, containing formulas for the feasts *Corporis Christi, Erici (Vespers), and Sabbato ante Domin. I. Augusti.*

Principal Kinds of Variants in Manuscript Sources

From the manuscript mentioned, I have chosen the antiphons 4 and 5 for Vespers compared to versions in other, more ordinary sources, in order to exemplify some different kinds of melodic variants. See Examples 1, 2 and 3.

The texts are, like most other chants for St. Erik from the same original form of the office, in Leonine (rhymed) hexameters. It is notable, and emphasized by the variants, that in both these antiphons the cadence does not follow the metre and text rhyme, but the syntax and meaning of the text, i.e. after *es* and *festa* respectively:

---

8 Treitler 1974, p. 344 (after F. Bartlett, *Remembering: A Study in Experimental and Social Psychology* (1932/R1972).
9 In the Swedish National Archives, Stockholm. Description in Moberg 1947, p. 99 f. Moberg emphasized the problem with the hymn melody. In his opinion, the text of the rubric—"[...] *cuius sacrum corpus in Vpsalensi ecclesia requiescit*"—would indicate an Uppsala provenance, although the fragment has served as wrapping on an lodger of accounts for the landscape of Småland.

Dulcis amice Dei[,] per quem rex magnificatus
es[,] clementer ei pro nobis funde precatus. Alleluia.
(Blissful friend of God, raised by Him to be king,
of your goodness pray to Him for us. Alleluia.)
Da Deus ut mitis regis[,] cuius veneramur
festa[,] piis meritis sanctis iungi mereamur. Alleluia.
(Grant, O Lord, for the sake of the gentle king
whose feast we celebrate, that we may also be found worthy to live with the saints. Alleluia.)[10]

a) *Text underlay.* Treitler describes the melodic movement as "moving through tonal space": the same melody only takes different linguistic sounds. See Ex. 1/VA 4: ANT 26 "amice", "clementer" and Ex. 2/VA 5 "veneramur", "iungi", "mereamur";

b) Intervals might be filled in by stepwise movement.

c) Contracting or enlarging of the *ambitus* of a formula. ANT 26 seems to avoid the highest or lowest notes, contracting the melody, thus making the *ambitus* smaller. See Ex. 1/VA 4 (ANT 26) "per … magnificatus".

The ambitus of formulas might also be enlarged: see VA 5, *festa,* and *cuius* in Ex. 3.

d) Shortening or prolongation of melismas—sometimes by repetition of melodic formulas. See ANT 26 in Ex. 1/VA 4 "de-i" (prol.:); "rex", "Alleluia" (abbr.:); and in Ex. 2/VA 5 "Da", "cuius".

e) Notational devices such as liquescences or composed neums (repeat of pitch), occur, especially with consonants such as l, m, n *(semivocales),* and diphtongs like au, ui, etc., e.g. in the word *alleluia.* Composed neums often occur at cadences. See Ex. 3: VA 5 "cuius" and Ex. 1, *magnificatus; precatus;* Ex. 2: *ut, mereamur.*

f) Clef errors and transpositions *ex parte:* such "scribal errors" might be due to astigmaticism (writing on the wrong line). In other cases, they can be explained as representing a use of semitones not belonging to the mode *(musica ficta).* See Ex. 1: VA 4 "per quem rex … ei", a passage where ANT 26 makes a new version, just like writing from (insufficient) memory.—Other "transpositions" are found in the Gospel antiphons *Miles regis* and *Corona fulgens.*[11]

---

10 Translation: Roger Tanner & Neil Betteridge.
11 These chants are discussed in my paper presented at the 11th Musica Antiqua Europae Orientalis conference in Bydgoszcz, Poland, 11–14 September 1997 (to be published).

g) The melodic movement within an interval is inversed: rising instead of falling, or *vice versa*. See Ex. 2/VA 5 ANT 26: "[venera]-mur".

h) Some variants may be due simply to the process of perception, memorization and/or remembering. See Ex. 2/VA 5 ANT 26 "alleluia"; VA 4 "per quem … es".

Example 1: VA 4
VA 4: *Dulcis amice dei* according to mss KB A 96, Gummerus I:3 and ANT 26/A 103 k 139.

When nothing is notated in the staffs for KB A 96 and ANT 26, it means that they give the same version as Gummerus I:3, the version chosen as a main source for the edition. It is a good representative of a stable tradition, and many other sources are closely similar to it. However, in this source only, the passage *"per quem … ei"* is transposed down by a second (notated "in F"). If performed as notated it would sound like A 96, with the exception of *"rex"*, where the semitone interval would differ, and of the descending movements at *"-ca-tus est"*. A 96 is from the same period, late 15th century. It is very similar to Gummerus I:3. However, it is presented here because the passage *"per quem rex […] ei"* is written at the same high pitch as in most other sources. Three early sources, however, write part of it, *"magnificatus … ei"*, like Gummerus I:3.

The scribe of ANT 26 seems to have been well aware of tonality, so the version of the same passage is not due to writing on the wrong line of the staff but seem to depend on an effort to remember the melody and write something similar to what he had heard, in the same mode and cadencing on the fundamental note. Also the Alleluia differs from the other sources.—Repeat of a formula at *de-i;* text underlay at *a-mi-ce*.

The *"rex"* melisma is shorter in some sources, longer in other ones.

Example 2: VA 5
VA 5 *Da deus* according to Gummerus I:3; ANT 26/Ak139 and some variants in other mss.

Example 2 shows versions in Gummerus I:3 (main source) and ANT 26. The "other mss" represented on the third staff are: *Da:* HUB ant 124, *ut:* "K 102",[12] *ve-ne[ramur]:* "K 102", *[venera]mur:* ULA fragm. 49, *fes[ta]:* "K 102", *iun-gi:* HUB ant 124, *me-re-a-mur:* "K 102".
piis: in all sources (without exception) the melodic movement is c->a->d, some sources doubling the initial note c.
Alleluia: some sources have "aha[a] G" instead of "ah aG".

---

[12] "K 102" is Moberg's operational term (1947) for the antiphoner filio serving as wrapping on the account books "Besvärsböcker 1610–1616".

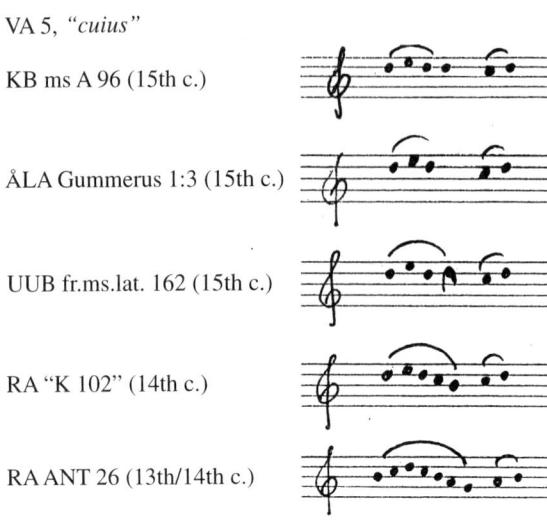

Example 3

The hymn melody shows several bipuncta (repercussive notes), written with *semivocales,* i.e. the same syllables of the text where liquescences are motivated.[13] But this source does not have the usual melody for the ordinary hymn texts. Moberg comments (1947): "ernste Schwierigkeiten bereitet aber die Erklärung der hier benutzten, für die Weihnachtszeit typischen Melodie 208, die [...] in den anderen Quellen der Erik-Hymnen durch die volkstümliche lydische Dominikanerweise M 247 ersetzt worden ist".

Concluding Remarks

In some sources, we find questions more often than answers. ANT 26 is one link in the tradition. Notwithstanding the poor quality of this source—the work of a seemingly awkward scribe, who maybe did not even remember the "correct" hymn melody—we can find it useful as an example of perception and memoration in medieval reality.

There might also be conclusions to be drawn concerning medieval transmission, ways of singing, and performance practice, as well as conclusions about how much of the sounded music is explicitly written down in the notation and what was regarded as implied/implicit and did not need to be prescribed.

13 Nilsson 1992, p. 81–83.

We can without doubt say that there were different manners of performing chant, more or less "correct" ways, especially before written tradition became the norm, taking over from the oral tradition. In my opinion, it is useful for singers to know where liquescences occur, and to know about medieval attitudes to written music and the conception of melody as "the voice singing the syllables of speech and [...] moving through the soundspace".[14] Similarly the editor, who has to choose a "best version", must consider the consequence of "canonizing" one sole version.

Depending on the aim of the research, different attitudes would be relevant regarding plainchant: "opus" or "living tradition", product or process. The testimony of different sources might be regarded as pieces in a jigsaw puzzle, or parts of a network encompassing more than one sole office.

Sources

Approximately 60 sources have been used for the forthcoming edition. Of these, only those mentioned in the text above are listed below.

Uppsala
The Regional Archives (*Landsarkivet,* ULA): Fragment nr 49, 15th century

Stockholm
The Royal Library (*Kungliga Biblioteket,* KB): Ms A 96
Fragment ANT 26 (A 103 k 139, presently in the National Archives), late 13th–early 14th century

The Swedish National Archives (*Riksarkivet,* RA): fragments
ANT 161, 15th century
"K 102" (shelf mark "Besvärsböcker 1610–1616"), 14th century

Skara
The Diocesan and School Library: Skara music manuscript no. 1, early 16th century

Åbo/Turku
Turun Maakuntaarkisto/Åbo Landsarkiv (ÅLA):
Gummerus I:3, 15th century
Gummerus I:5, late 15th–early 16th century

Helsinki/Helsingfors
Helsinki University Library (HUB), fragm. ms. lat.
ant. 28, 14th century
ant 124, (late 14th)–early 15th century

---

14 Treitler 1984, p. 145.

Literature

AH, *Analecta hymnica medii aevi* vol. 25 (1897), ed. Blume, p. 285–288.

Haapanen 1927, Toivo Haapanen, "Olika skikt i S:t Eriks metriska officium". Nordisk Tidskrift för Bok- och Biblioteksforskning XIV/1927, p. 53–83.

Hiley 1993, David Hiley, "Constitution, objectives and activities". *International Musicological Society Study Group Cantus planus. Papers read at the 6th meeting, Eger, Hungary, 1993*, vol. 2, p. 855–858.

Moberg 1947, Carl-Allan Moberg, *Die liturgischen Hymnen in Schweden* I (1947).

Moberg–Nilsson 1991, Carl-Allan Moberg & Ann-Marie Nilsson, *Die liturgischen Hymnen in Schweden* II:1–2 (1991).

Nilsson 1990, Ann-Marie Nilsson, "A Hymn in 'Hystorie' for Swedish Saints". *International Musicological Society Study Group Cantus planus. Papers read at the Third Meeting, Tihany, Hungary, 19–24 September 1988* (Budapest 1990), p. 165–180.

Nilsson 1992, Ann-Marie Nilsson, "Adest dies leticie: Studies on hymn melodies in medieval Sweden". *Proceedings of the First British-Swedish Conference on Musicology. Medieval studies, 11–15 May 1988*. Ed. Ann Buckley (Publication issued by the Royal Swedish Academy of Music no. 71, 1992), p. 67–85.

Treitler 1974, Leo Treitler, "Homer and Gregory: the transmission of epic poetry and plainchant", *Musical Quarterly* 1974, p. 372–333.

Treitler 1984, Leo Treitler, "Reading and singing: on the genesis of Occidental music-writing". *Early Music Studies in Medieval and Early Modern Music 4* (1984).

Thordeman 1954, Bengt Thordeman (ed.), *Erik den helige. Historia—kult—reliker.* Studier utgivna under red. av Bengt Thordeman (1954). [Articles by K.G. Westman and Toni Schmid.]

The Early Liturgy of St Olav

Eyolf Østrem

Some time during the years 1161–1189 archbishop Eystein, the second archbishop of Nidaros, wrote or compiled a complete proper office for St Olav, the patron saint of the newly established Norwegian church province. It was a full-scale office, which met all the needs for a feast of the highest rank, with a matins of nine lessons as the crowning point. This office was used all over Scandinavia throughout the medieval period, until the reformation rendered it obsolete, and it is amply represented in the sources. But between Olav's death at Stiklestad and the writing of the new office lie 150 years, and the picture of this period is less clear.

The liturgical side of this early period of the church is rarely discussed in modern historical writing. In the more general presentations it is merely presupposed that there were specific texts in current use. The most recent general history of Norway states: "Already in the 1030's the norwegian church started celebrating the Olav mass. In that connection the church needed purely liturgical texts and a short saint's vita which described the king's life and death" (Krag 1995:126). Some authors (e.g. Gunnes 1996) go into this more in detail, and these texts are specified as the so called *Translatio Sancti Olavi*—a liturgical text describing the events surrounding his translation and canonization in 1031, and a complete office in current use also in Norway from 1050 or earlier: named the *Leofric Office* after the donor of the book in which it is found.[1] Together with the extended pilgrimage, this would make up a complete, liturgical celebration. It is my intention in this article to modify this picture.

The celebration of St Olav as a saint and martyr began immediately after his death at Stiklestad in 1030, according to the sagas. It has been described in various sources how the english missionary bishop Grimkell moved the body to

---

1 See e.g. Gunnes 1995, Gjerløw 1967.

Nidaros 1 year and 5 days after his death. At that time the body had more or less crawled out of the ground by itself, according to Snorri Sturlasson.

Between that time and the age of archbishop Eystein there are practically no traces of St Olav in the Norwegian sources. The diplomatic sources are practically silent. Adam of Bremen, writing ca. 1070, mentions a letter from Adalbert, archbishop of Hamburg, reproaching king Harald Hardråde for using the gifts to the shrine of St Olav for military purposes (RegNorv 1 nr. 42; Adam III:17). Somewhat later (ca. 1105) the three Magnusson kings—Sigurd (Jorsalfare), Øystein and Olav—confirm in a letter certain rights from the days of St Olav (RegNorv 1 nr. 56). Apart from these two documents, the first traces of St Olav in diplomas are from the time after 1153, and generally directly connected with the archsee or the kingdom itself. Letters have been lost, of course, but this hundred-years silence is noteworthy, nevertheless.

Some skaldic poems were written within ten years of Olav's death,[2] but even that is a dying branch. It was partly re-vitalized with the celebratory poem "Geisli", written for the establishment of the archdiocese in 1153, but that was a special—and singular—occurrence.

No iconographical evidence exists from this early age. A few coins from the age of Olav Haraldsson have been preserved, but the images on these are typified king's images, no portraits (cf. Lidén 1997:26). Apart from these, the icon in the Church of Nativity in Bethlehem is the first depiction of the saint. It can be securely dated to the 1150s or 60s, and also this icon can be directly connected with the archsee.[3]

Grimkell and the Early St Olav Cult in England

We must instead turn to England for the earliest traces of a liturgical celebration of St Olav. In a letter dating from around 1050–60 a certain "Gyða comitissa" gives her lands in Scireford to a church of "Sancti Olavi regis et martyris" for

---

2 Most important are Thorarin Lovtunga's "Glælognskvida" and Sigvat skald's "Erfidrápa". Glælognskvida was originally written in honor of the danish king Svein Alfivason, but it contains an extended passage describing Olav and how his hair and nails kept growing after his death, and that blind and deaf were cured at his shrine. The poems were dated 1032 and 1038 respectively by Finnur Jónsson (1908–12:251, 324ff).

3 Bruce Dickins (1940:64 and plate facing p. 60) has dated the Herringfleet-seal from Stafford to the 12th century, which would make it equally old or older than the Bethlehem icon. This dating is however disputable (I am grateful to Anne Lidén for this information).

her and her husband earl Godwin's souls,[4] and in a letter from 1063 king Edward (the confessor) mentions a donation of land "for the salvation of his soul" to a church of St Olav, which has been built on land which he has donated.[5] According to *The Anglo-Saxon Chronicle* an Olav's church had been built in York by Siward, the danish Earl of York. This must have been done some time before 1055, which was when Siward died.[6] These are the earliest churches dedicated to St Olav for which there is direct evidence. They were followed by numerous others.

From the same time—the years around 1050—are the oldest liturgical sources related to St Olav. The known sources of the early St Olav's liturgy in England are:[7]

- A litany for the dedication of a church, from Exeter or Ramsey, first half of the 11th c. (GB-Lbl, Cotton Vitellius AVII fol. 18);
- A litany in the "Leofric Psalter", donated to the Exeter cathedral by bishop Leofric (GB-Lbl Harley 863, fol 109v);
- A litany from Exeter *(The Exeter Pontifical)* from the second half of the 11th c. (GB-Lbl, Add. 28.188, fol 3).
- The Red Book of Darley (Cambridge CCC 422) from ca 1050–60, which contains the three mass prayers.
- The Leofric Collectar (GB-Lbl, Harley 2961), ca. 1050.

---

4 Chartae Anglosaxonicae 926. "Ego Gyða comitissa concedo ecclesie sancti Olavi regis et martyris terram meam de scireford, quae est de dote mea, pro anima mea et domini mei comitis Godwini." "I, countess Gyða, concede my land in Scireford, which belongs to my dowry, to a church of saint Olav, king and martyr, for my soul and for the soul of my lord, count Godwin." The letter ends by summoning the "eternal torments of hell together with Judas the traitor" upon anyone who tries to take the land from the church.

5 Chartae Anglosaxonicae 814. Edward describes how he is being troubled by the unrest in the kingdom, and wants to remedy this, i.a. through endowments to churches. "Inspired by this, and begged by a priest called Scepius, I have donated a part of my land to Sta Maria and St Thomas Apostle, and St Olav, king and martyr, for whom a churc has been built on land that I have endowed," etc. "Hoc inspirante etiam, rogante quodam presbytero nomine Scepio, pro remedio animae meae donavi sanctae Mariae et sancto Thomae apostolo, ac sancto Olavo regi ac martyri, cui aecclesia quam terra dotavi constructa est, particulam praedii, *hoc est dimidiam virgam et dimidium quatrentem terrae in loco Kenebiri et Lan … dicto, eo tenore, ut amodo idem rus praedictae aecclesiae liberum ab omni censu et servicio subiaceat, ac presbytero qui eidem presit ecclesiae, serviat.*"—Dickins (1940:56) and A.O. Johnsen (1975:28) think that this is the same church as the one mentioned by Gyða. Unless the two villages mentioned in the letters, "Kenebiri" and "Scireford", can be shown to be related, there seems to be little in the letters themselves to support this interpretation, and neither Dickins nor Johnsen explain their view further.

6 "1055. Died Siward the Earl at York, an he lies buried at Galmanho, in the minster which he himself built and hallowed in God's and Olaf's name." *Anglo-Saxon Chron.* D. (Quoted from Metcalfe 1881:34).

7 See Iversen 1998 for a more comprehensive discussion of the liturgical contents of these early sources.

Most famous of these is the "Leofric Collectar" which contains the St Olav Office mentioned in the introduction. The three litanies only contain Olav's name listed among the other saints.

All these occurences of an english St Olav's cult can, in some way or another, be traced back to one man: Grimkell. Among the bishops brought to Norway from England by Olav, Grimkell is the only one left in Norway in 1031, and he is by all probability the author of the first office of St Olav as preserved in the Leofric collectar (Birkeli 1980; Johnsen 1975). It has long been known that there was a bishop Grimkillus in Selsey (i.e. Sussex, in the south-east corner of England) from 1038 to 1047, and already P.A. Munch, writing in the 1850s, considered it likely that the two 'Grimkell's were one and the same. This was certainly an interesting thought, but the evidence of a diploma signed by Grimkillus of Selsey as early as 1026 seemed to sweep away this theory. The historians settled with the loose hypothesis that the "Norwegian" Grimkillus after Olav's death continued his work in the eastern parts of Norway, where he had relatives. In 1898, however, it was proved that the charter from 1026 was a falsification, and there was really nothing which could speak against the theory of P. A. Munch after all.

And now the threads can be gathered: *Leofric* was bishop of Exeter and as such one of Grimkell's "colleagues". He had owned and probably compiled the Leofric Collectar. From Exeter are also the three litanies where St Olav's name first occurs in a litugical source, and Exeter is where Gyða's church is situated. A point of special interest is that the letter about her gift to the church is given authorization by the very same "Leofric Exoniensis episcopus". *Gyða and Godwin* are not just your average, happily married nobles—they were the most powerful family in England around the middle of the 11th century. *Siward of York* was the second most powerful of the earls, and all these men regularly gathered at the king's council. They have all witnessed royal letters together (see Barlow 1979 for a survey of the characters and institutions of the pre-conquest church in England). It seems likely that Grimkell had used his influence in this illustrious company to spread the cult that was already gaining a certain reputation—and which he himself had "created".

It can be worth mentioning that the traces of the english St Olav cult are not from the areas with a substantial Nordic/Norwegian population. To the contrary, they are mainly located in the south, where the Nordic element was the weakest. Birkeli argues that only an ecclesiastical origin can explain the spread of the St Olav office (Birkeli 1980:211). Thus the english cult can not be explained as a response to a demand from Nordic citizens in England. It is rather—if a poetic touch be permitted—a foreign rose, planted under favourable conditions, in a firmly established church organization, but which gradually disappeared when its gardener died.

Between Grimkell and Eystein

The Pilgrimage
The first hint at what was going on in Norway, is Adam of Bremen's report from the 1070s about the Nordic churches, where also the pilgrimage to Nidaros is mentioned. Adam writes (Adam, Book 4, ch. 33):

> Metropolis civitas nortmannorum est Trondemnis, quae nunc decorata ecclesiis, magna populorum frequentia celebratur. In qua iacet corpus beatissimi Olavi regis et martyris. Ad cuius tumbam usque in hodiernum diem maxima Dominus operatur sanitatum miracula, ita ut a longinquis illic regionibus confluant hii, qui se meritis sancti non desperant iuvari.

> The largest city of the Norwegians is Trondemnis; which today is adorned with churches and is often visited by big crowds. There rest the remains of St Olav, the blessed king and martyr. At his grave until this day the Lord works the greatest miracles of healing, so that people who do not lack the hope that they can be helped by the saint's merits, flock together there from distant lands.[8]

Adam had not been in Nidaros himself, but apparently his sources are reliable, at least if we allow for a slight qualification of the "distant lands". That there has been a cult, appears from other sources as well. It is mentioned in several of the sagas of Snorri, writing ca. 1230. In the Saga of Magnus the Good Snorri quotes this verse, written by Sigvat Skald:

> *Many a man, quickly mended,*
> *wends from the holy saint's sepulchre,*
> *and many, seeing*
> *who blind came there.*[9]

Apart from this, there are no direct sources to the pilgrimage before the time of Eystein. There are however some indirect sources from a later date, which seem to reflect an earlier practice. When king Sverre in 1179 approached Nidaros to conquer the city for the first time, he stopped at a place called "Feginsbrekka"

---

8 My translation. The words "metropolis civitas", which otherwise is mostly used about an arch-see, is, according to Nyberg (1984:333), by Adam often used to denote the largest city or "capital" in areas without specific bishoprics (Trondheim, Lund, Kiev and indirectly about Birka and Rethra).
9 ch. 10; Hollander 1964:548.

and knelt in prayer (Sverres saga, ch. 35). Feginsbrekka is a mountain hill in present-day Byåsen, the hillside to the south of Nidaros which one has to cross to reach the city. The name means "The Mountain of Joy" and is often described in very general terms, as the place where "the pilgrims could first see the city with its churches and towers, and expressed their joy and gratitude to God" (Blom 1965). The interpretation can however be narrowed down considerably. Erik Gunnes has pointed out that "Feginsbrekka" is a direct translation of "Montjoie", which originally was the pilgrims' name for Monte Mario to the north of Rome, but soon both Jerusalem and Santiago de Compostela, had their own "Montjoie"s (Gunnes 1996:177). This clearly indicates that at the time of Sverre's conquest (if the saga can be trusted at this point) the cult of St Olav was far-reaching enough to be compared to and modeled upon the three major sites of pilgrimage in the christian world.[10]

The document known as "Magnus Erlingssons privilegiebrev" (letter of privilege to the church), most probably from 1163,[11] states that pilgrims to Nidaros shall enjoy full royal protection, even if they should come from countries otherwise at war with Norway, and that anyone who violates a pilgrim will be banned from the realm (RN 1, 145; edited in Vandvik 1959). Similar decrees were issued by later kings.

Finally the church had an interest in an extensive cult, since it generated income to the church and to the city. In 1169 the archbishop was granted the privilege of giving a certain indulgence to pilgrims (RN 1, 128).

All this attests to the importance and size of the pilgrimage to St Olav around the middle of the 12th century. But when asked what happened once the pilgrims had reached Nidaros, the sources have less to say.

The "Translatio Sancti Olavi"

In Theodoric's *History of the ancient Norwegian Kings*, dating from ca. 1180, and hence one of the earliest historical texts on Norway, Theodoric writes about the translation:

> Hec omnia a nonnullis memorie tradita sunt, nos notis immorari superfluum duximus (Ch. XX; Storm 1880:44).
>
> *All these [i.e. the events surrounding the translation] have been brought to memory by several [authors], wherefore we find it unnecessary to dwell any longer on these well known facts.*

---

10 The Octogon in the cathedral of Nidaros itself was probably constructed as a copy of the Grave Church in Jerusalem (see for instance Danbolt 1997:108ff).

11 This is the year the child-king Magnus Erlingsson was crowned. For a further discussion of the dating of the letter, see Gunnes 1996:118.

When G. Storm edited the text in 1880 he read this as a reference to a liturgical "Translatio Sancti Olavi", to be used at the translation feast of St Olav (August 3rd). This text must then, according to Storm, have been lost along the way, since the legend written by Eystein was used also for the Translatio feast in the printed Breviarium Nidrosiense of 1519, which would otherwise have been the natural place for this hypothetical text (Storm 1880:44).

This seems to be reading too much into the passage. I can see no obvious reasons for this assumption and take the passage to mean nothing more than what Theodoricus actually writes: that the events surrounding the translation have been described by other authors—skalds and chroniclers—and probably even that it was commonly known what happened in 1031, so that is was unnecessary to include yet another account of this in his historical work. Similar passages occur elsewhere, e.g. in Adam's writings, as an excuse for not recounting the whole story. That Theodoricus should refer to a specifically *liturgical* text is not even hinted at, and this supposition should be treated with caution, if not discarded altogether.[12]

The Grimkell Office in Norway

It has generally been held that the office which Grimkell wrote was used in Norway until the 1160s or '70s, when it was completely superseded by Eystein's new office. Three of the collect prayers and the three antiphons in this office which specifically mention Olav must have been preserved in some form or another, since they are used as alternative songs for the days of the octave in the printed Breviarium Nidrosiense of 1519, which contains the most comprehensive version of the "Eystein"-office. This has been taken as proof that "the Leofric office was used in Nidaros before it was superseded by the Eystein-office. It is possible that it never went out of use in Nidaros proper, but was sung during the octave as in the breviary, although this cannot be documented" (Gjerløw 1967: col. 566).[13] The Leofric office was mainly based upon elements from the

---

12 Interestingly enough Gunnes in his recent book on Eystein discusses the hypothetical *Translatio*, but without reference to Theodoricus. His reasons to believe in the existance of such a work are a) possible traces of it in the Legendary Saga, b) possible traces of insertions in Theodoricus' book, "which might come from a work like this", c) that the celebratory "Geisli" from 1153 seems to be based upon a tradition (Gunnes 1995:207f). This seems to be weak evidence.
13 "[U]tgjør beviset for at Leofric-officiet var i bruk i Nidaros før det ble avløst av Øystein-officiet. Det er mulig at de aldri gikk av bruk i selve Nidaros men ble sunget under oktaven som i breviariet, skjønt det kan ikke dokumenteres" (sp 566).

commune sanctorum and does hardly relate directly to the saint. The new office would then have been written in response to a growing demand for an office which emphasized the saint more strongly.

The case is more complex than it may seem, and I will spend some time on another hypothesis: that during the first century after Stiklestad the feast of St Olav has been celebrated using the common liturgy for a saint, the *Commune unius martyris*.

The Common in a Loosely Organized Province

The simplest argument for this is of course that this was common practice—after all, that was what the *commune sanctorum* was there for in the first place. Gunilla Iversen has shown how the Leofric office is based upon texts drawn from the *commune sanctorum* and argues that this was the necessary procedure to establish a new saint as a proper, "correct" saint: "In the first step of establishing the King as a saint, it seems clear that the most important issue was not to write new texts, but rather to make the right choice of already existing texts used for the celebration of well established prestigious royal saints" (Iversen 1998).

The recourse to the *commune* must have been especially useful for a church province as loosely and randomly organized as the Norwegian in the first century or so after St Olav's death. No clearly delineated bishoprics existed before Olav Kyrre (king of Norway 1066–93); his Christ-churches in Nidaros and in Bergen were apparently conceived as episcopal churches (Johnsen 1955:10; Danbolt 1997:26f), but these are isolated—and probably somewhat premature—instances. Throughout the rest of the country and some time into the 12th century the structure must have been very loose. In this loose structure the responsibility for the existing churches was shared by the relatively few bishops and priests, who ambulated between churches rather than being stationary at one place. Most priests and bishops in Norway during the first century were foreigners—englishmen, but from the middle of the century, when the contacts with Bremen stabilized, more and more germans—who were taught in their own liturgical traditions, who brought their own liturgical books with them to the country and to the churches they visited. The chances for a new office like the Grimkell-office to find its way into this maze and establish itself throughout Norway, seem to be slim.[14] It can be argued that this is not probable until a fixed chapter church has been established, where the training of new priests can

---

14 It might be argued that the english priests may have brought the "Leofric Office" with them from England. This may of couse have happened—however unlikely this is if the office spread as locally in England as it seems—but it would nevertheless still only be isolated occurences.

be accomplished. The soil was far better prepared in England, and even there it took the lucky circumstance of a bishop like Leofric, with a special interest in books, for the Grimkell office to be preserved in a liturgical book.

The *commune sanctorum* is a basic repository even for the establishment of a new liturgy. Gunilla Iversen points out in her forthcoming article (1998) that "newness" is not on the agenda in such a case—to the contrary, it was important to emphasise that the new office stands on solid, traditional ground. And hence it is no surprise that the liturgical texts that were chosen for the first office of St Olav are generally drawn from the *commune,* or from the offices of earlier english king saints. In fact, even the last responsory of the "Eystein" office, *Rex inclitus,* which has been used to suggest a link with St Denis (Bergsagel 1976:15), has a direct model also in the *Commune unius martyris* in York and Durham.

The Sagas

The sagas have remarkably little to tell us about the cult of St Olav in the first century after his death. The sagas' main interest is to describe the actions of the kings, thus being heavily biased in favor of warfare, direct (and often bloody) diplomacy, and—in the case of the enigmatic Olav Kyrre—even administration. But even though much may have happened which has not reached the chronicles, one does certainly not get the impression that either Magnus the good or his uncle, the extremely hard-headed, strategical, tyrant/warrior-king Harald Hardråde, were particularly interested in ecclesiastical matters. Only one chapter in the sagas of these kings contains a reference to the cult of St Olav. Ch. 10 of the saga of Magnus the Good, where the pilgrimage is mentioned (see above p. 47), also contains a description of the shrine which Magnus had made for his father's holy body. After this description the saga continues (ch. 10; Unger 1868:523, Hollander 1964:548):

> Þá var þat í lög tekit um allan Noreg at halda heilagt hátíð Ólafs konungs, var þá sá dagr þegar þar svá haldinn, sem hinar œztu hátíðr. Þess getr Sigvatr Skáld:
>
> Oss dugir Olafs messo
> iofur magnar guð fagna
> meinalaus i mino
> Magnus föður húsi.
>
> *Then it was written into the laws everywhere in Norway that the memorial day of King Ólaf was to be kept holy. And then that day was kept as holy as the greatest of festivals. This is mentioned by the skald Sigvat:*

It behooves us to hold e'er
holy—God has given
power to sainted prince—with
pure spirit his mass day.[15]

This mentions specifically the Olav's mass and more generally states that St Olav's day was to be celebrated as a feast of the highest rank.

As rare as this passage is, it opens up some interesting questions regarding the possibility of an office in continuous use. It seems from the context of this quotation that the celebration of St Olav's day is decreed by Magnus, the king, and not by any ecclesiastical authority; it follows immediately upon an enumeration of Magnus' actions concerning his father's body and shrine. However this may be, it points to the intrigueing possibility that this is mainly the expression of the son's piety towards his father, rather than just the king's piety towards a saint. But it also reflects the position of the church at the time, as an institution closely connected with the king. At the time of Magnus (and even more of Olav), before the first wave of reform around the middle of the century, the national churches were generally at the hands of the kings (Barlow 1979:4f). In Scandinavia the royal influence over the church was even more pronounced, as the national church was only recently established and still must have depended upon the power and goodwill of the kingdom—which had established it in the first place—to survive. One can perhaps even ask: was there anyone at all, apart from the king, in the years after Olav's death with the authority to decree the use of a new office in Norway? The evidence of the St Olav's churches which were established in Denmark by Magnus, points in the same direction. Tore Nyberg has recently argued that these were not consecrated to St Olav as a result of the popularity of the cult, but by royal decree (Nyberg 1997).

One more point is worth making. Sigvat Skald's strophe in the quotation from the Saga of Magnus the Good above mentions the mass only, and in a way that could even suggest a private, devotional mass, not a national celebration of the patron saint. ("In my house I will celebrate Olav's mass"). Practicing some kind of cult in immediate connection with royal houses or houses of local authorities was the rule rather than the exception, both in pre-christian and christian times. The royal halls were the site for the *official* cult, and this could have been the content of Sigvat's strophe, if it weren't for the word *"hus"*, which in old norse is only used to denote a small house or room, and never a hall of this

---

15 A more exact translation would be: "We should celebrate the mass of Olav, whom God has given power, the father of Magnus, with pure spirit, in my house."

kind. This means that what Sigvat has in mind is most likely a private celebration of some kind.[16] This brings up the question if one should make a distinction between the *mass* and the *office*. Could the mass have been celebrated from the start, privately and/or in royal churches, without being accompanied by the larger office? The mass was the most important celebration during the day, but the main event from the point of view of a saint (or rather: the saint's followers …) was the office. The office contains the proper songs and the legend. The elements of the mass proper to the saint of the day, on the other hand, are few—the prayers, which usually were the same at mass as in the office, the verse of the alleluia, and the sequence—and it would have been easier to accomplish this at an early stage, than the more extended proper elements of the office. The collect prayers would then have been retained, whereas the rest would have been supplied from the *Commune sanctorum*. It is noteworthy that these are exactly the elements which have been preserved from the Leofric Office in the newer office, whereas the elements pertaining exclusively to the office—i.e. antiphons and responsories—have not been found in newer sources.

Judging from the sagas, the kingdom seems to have had no particular interest in a cult of St Olav after the time of the closest relatives, Magnus and Harald, and the church, which, mainly because of the pilgrimage, retained its interest, may have lacked the means. Not until the establishment of the archbishopric of Nidaros and of Norway as an independent church province was the need for a more advanced liturgy for the patron saint felt strongly enough, at the same time as the church had far better possibilities to accomplish this.

This view gains support from the *Ordo nidrosiensis ecclesie,* the summary of the entire liturgy of the province, set down in the early 13th century. For the celebration at St Olav's day it specifies lessons as follows:

> "*Lectiones de passione eius in .i.° et .ij.° legatur nocturno vel sermo de uno martyre*"
>
> ("Lessons from his passion [i.e. the *Passio Olavi*] are to be read at the first and second nocturn, or the lessons for a martyr [i.e. from the *commune sanctorum*].") (Gjerløw 1968:372).

This is not a concession to freedom of choice, but rather an acknowledgement that not all churches within the province had this special text for St Olav. When it is not considered certain that all churches have this text at this late date, how can we suppose an office like the Grimkell-office to have spread beyond Nidaros two hundred years earlier? The passage from the *Ordo* also illustrates what

---

16 I am grateful to Olof Sundquist for pointing out the interpretational possibilities in this choice of words.

we have already said: that it was common practice to supply from the *commune* what was not otherwise at hand.

The Early Sources and Adam of Bremen
There are other sources too, bringing evidence against a widespread, strong proper liturgy of St Olav. One is Adam of Bremen, the "court chronicler" of the see of Hamburg/Bremen, writing in the 1070's. Adam relates the history of the see itself and of its provinces, and officially Nidaros and the rest of the Nordic countries belonged to this see. Concerning Olav, Adam has no hard sources at his disposal; his description is based upon reports from colleagues and from the danish king Svein Estridsson, the adversary of the two kings of the Olav-dynasty, Magnus and Harald. Bremen was at this time very eager to emphasize its major role in the mission in the north, and this is one of the chief aims of Adam's book. Vera Henriksen has pointed out in her book about St Olav, that had there existed liturgical writings about Olav at this point, they would have been available in the metropolitan church in Bremen, and Adam would have known about them. That he apparently has had no such sources at hand, implies, according to Henriksen, *e silentio* that they may not either have existed. Conclusions of this kind must of course be treated with caution, but it is still an interesting argument, given the closer contacts between Nidaros and Bremen in the second half of the 11th century.

Several early fragments of litugical books found in the Swedish State Archive which mention Olav, can be dated to the time before or around Eystein's office. The oldest, probably from the first half of the 12th century, is probably even the oldest evidence of a liturgical celebration of St Olav in Scandinavia (CCM Br 1269). Disappointingly enough, his name is just incorporated in the collect prayer for other saints of the day, and that is all there is to it. Not even a proper prayer. Recently two fragments of another codex dating from the middle or late 12th century have turned up in the swedish State Archive (Fr 1681–1682). Even this codex contains Olav's name in a collect prayer in the same manner as in the previous source. It could be argued that since these are Swedish sources they can not be expected to reflect the newest developments of a Norwegian saint. This could be part of the reason for their limited scope, but on the other hand there are numerous early, and comprehensive, swedish sources for the Eystein-office—the earliest are probably from the years around 1200 and so postdating the earlier sources only by a few decades—so the conclusion, albeit tentative, may perfectly well be that no specific office or set of prayers have been generally available before Eystein wrote his office.

All in all it seems to be wise to regard the new office in the light of the church-political situation at the middle of the 12th century. Before 1153 the cult of St Olav may have served as an important argument in favour of Nidaros in the struggle to get the archbishop-see of the planned Norwegian province. Even though Nidaros was Norway's largest city, it was not an obvious choice: its location far to the north must have felt slightly impractical, and Bergen was already established as an important commercial city, with a cathedral of the same kind as Olav Kyrre's Christ Church in Nidaros.[17] If there was no widespread, proper liturgical cult of St Olav already, this must have seemed an appropriate time to search the ecclesiastical archives for information on the saint.

It is also likely that new texts had been produced in the decades around 1150. The dominant position of the Eystein office makes it difficult to trace any of this, but the writings of Theodoricus and the other historians, as well as Geisli, can be considered as results of this process. Three breviary fragments in the Swedish State Archive are interesting in this respect. The oldest (Br 258, from the latter part of the 12th century) has lessons taken from Eystein's *Passio Olavi,* but unique chants, not to be found in any other source. The texts of the chants are directly related to St Olav, but they have nothing to do with Eystein's text. The other source consists of two bifolios from a fragmented breviary (Fr 596 and Fr 614), a century younger. It has the opposite pattern: the common songs, but a unique legend text for the lessons. The chant texts of the first source are directly related to this new legend text, which means that this text must date from the end of the 12th century—about the same time as Eystein's legend—or even earlier.[18]

This evidence makes it tempting to ask if these songs and texts cannot originally have been part of the Grimkell office; the source containing the unique chants is itself one of the earliest records of Eystein's text, which indicates an old age even for the other items. And since the Grimkell office is found in an collectarium, which mainly lists the prayers and not the songs, one can not be certain that the Leofric Collectar contains all the songs that ever belonged to the office. Any "odd" songs found in more recent sources could be missing elements of the first office. This can hardly be more than a hypothesis, and several facts speak against it: that the Leofric Collectar in fact does include songs; that the contents of the legend found in Fr596/Fr614 seems to point to the 12th rather than the 11th century, and that there is, as Iversen points out, no reason to

---

17 I am grateful to Nils Holger Pedersen for discussing this with me.
18 These sources will be discussed more thoroughly in a forthcoming article.

expect a full-fledged office at such an early date. One may even add that other sources too contain extra songs, and there is a limit to how many missing songs we may assume. A more cautious hypothesis is that the unique songs and legend text may just as well be the outcome of a period of experimenting with new texts—and songs—for what had now turned out to be the most important saint in northern christendom. The two older sources, where St Olav's name is just mentioned in another saint's prayer, also point in this direction: to the gradual development of a liturgical "Olav-consciousness" during the 12th century rather than an extended celebration from 1030.

The aim of this article has been to show that the mere *existence* of an office does not necessarily mean that it has been commonly *used*. The arguments can be summarized as follows: a) The institutional foundation was weak; the church, which may have had the interest, lacked the power, and the kingdom, which controlled the church, seems to have showed more interest in the memory of the king himself than in liturgy. b) There was no fixed church organization, few priests and no centralized liturgy. c) The earliest liturgical sources from Scandinavia show no clear signs of a proper office being used in the area, as one might also expect. d) Whereas the early pilgrimage seems to be undisputable, that is not the case with the so called *"Translatio Sancti Olavi"*. e) A distinction may be drawn between the mass and the office.

After 1153 the cult becomes even more important, because of the new role of St Olav: as eternal king, feudal lord, maybe even eternal bishop,[19] and above all: national patron saint, generally celebrated throughout Scandinavia. The fact that St Olav's city is now even the seat of an archbishop and head of the Norwegian church province, makes the cult of St Olav all the more important. But this is a role and a situation which is new around the middle of the 12th century.

---

19 According to evidence presented by Anne Lidén in her forthcoming dissertation (Lidén 1998).

References

Sources

GB – British Museum
    Cotton Vitellius AVII fol. 18 (Litany from Exeter or Ramsey)
    Harley 863, fol 109v (Litany in the Leofric Psalter)
    Add. 28.188, fol 3 (Litany in the Exeter Pontifical), edited in Dewick/Frere 1914–21
    Harley 2961 (The Leofric Collectar), edited in Dewick/Frere 1914–21

GB – Cambridge
    CCC 422 ("The red book of Darley")

S – Svenska Riksarkivet (SRA)
    Fragm. Stockholm
        Fr 1681 (KA Västergötland 1602:7:1)
        Fr 1682 (KA Västergötland 1602:7:2)
        Fr 596 (Östergötland 1598:8:2)
        Fr 614 (Östergötland 1599:6:3)
    CCM (Catalogus Codicum Mutilorum)
        Br 258 (Östergötland 1586:7)
        Br 1269 (Småland 1559:3 avtaget, folioserien)

Adam of Bremen, *Gesta hammaburgensis ecclesie pontificum*. In *Monumenta Germaniae Historia. Scriptores* VII, Hannover, 1846. Swedish translation and edition by Emanuel Svenberg, Stockholm: Proprius, 1984.

Breviarium Nidrosiense, printed 1519. Facsimile edition 1964, Oslo: Børsums forlag.

Chartae Anglosaxonicae = Kemble, John M. (ed.) 1839–48, *Codex diplo-maticus Aevi Saxonici*, London.

DN = Diplomatarium Norvegicum (1849–). Oslo: Norsk Historisk Kjeldeskrift-Institutt.

Hollander, Lee M. (ed.) (1964), *Heimskringla, history of the kings of Norway by Snorri Sturluson*, Austin: University of Texas press.

RegNorv = *Regesta Norvegica* (1978–), Oslo: Norsk Historisk Kjeldeskrift-Institutt.

Sverres Saga. *Noregs Kongesoger, Jubileumsutgåva 1979*, vol. 3, Oslo: Det Norske Samlaget.

Unger, C.R. (ed) (1868): *Heimskringla eller Norges Kongesagaer af Snorre Sturlassøn*, Christiania (Oslo): Brøgger & Christie.

Literature

Barlow, Frank (1979), *The English Church 1000–1066*, 2. ed., London/New York: Longman.

Bergsagel, John (1976), "Liturgical relations between England and Scandinavia: as seen in selected musical fragments from the 12th and 13th centuries", in *Nordisk Kollokvium IV for Latinsk liturgiforskning*.

Birkeli, Fridtjov (1980), "Biskop Grimkell og Hellig-Olav". *Tidsskrift for teologi og kirke*, p. 109–130, 207–223.

Blom, Grethe Authén (1965), "Feginsbrekka". *Gyldendals store konversasjonsleksikon,* 2. ed., Oslo: Gyldendal.

Danbolt, Gunnar 1997, *Nidarosdomen,* Oslo.

Dewick, E. S./Frere, W. H. (ed.) (1914–21), *The Leofric Collectar* 1–2, London: Henry Bradshaw Society 45, 56.

Dickins, Bruce (1940), "The Cult of Saint Olave in the British Isles". *Saga-Book of the Viking Society for Northern Research* XII:2, London.

Gjerløw, Lilli (1967), "Olav den Hellige", in *Kulturhistorisk Leksikon for Nordisk Middelalder (KLNM)* 12, Oslo: Gyldendal.

Gjerløw, Lilli (1968), *Ordo Nidrosiensis Ecclesiae,* Oslo: Norsk Historisk Kjeldeskrift-Institutt.

Gunnes, Erik (1996), *Erkebiskop Eystein, statsmann og kirkebygger,* Oslo: Aschehoug.

Henriksen, Vera (1985), *Hellig-Olav,* Oslo: Aschehoug.

Iversen, Gunilla (1998), "Transforming a viking into a saint", in Rebecca A. Baltzer/Margot E. Fassler (eds.) *The Divine Office in the Latin Middle Ages: Methodology and Source Studies, Regional Developments,* Hagiography. Oxford: Oxford University Press.

Johnsen, Arne Odd (1955), "Fra den eldste tid til 1252", in *Nidaros erkebispestol og bispesete 1153–1953* Vol 1, Oslo: Forlaget land og kirke.

Johnsen, Arne Odd (1975), "Om misjonsbiskopen Grimkellus", *(Norsk) Historisk Tidskrift* 1975, p. 22–34.

Jónsson, Finnur (1912), *Den norsk–islandske Skjaldedigtning,* København/Kristiania (Oslo): Gyldendal.

Lidén, Anne (1997), "Bilden av Sankt Olav", in Lars Rumar (ed.), *Helgonet i Nidaros, Olavskult och Kristnande i Norden.*

Lidén, Anne (1998), *Olav den Helige i medeltida bildkonst.* Kungliga Vitterhets Historie och Antikvitets Akademien. Stockholm (in publication).

Krag, Claus (1995), *Vikingtid og rikssamling, Aschehougs norgeshistorie,* vol. 2, Oslo: Aschehoug.

Metcalfe, Frederic (1881), *Passio et Miracula Beati Olavi,* Oxford: Clarendon Press.

Noregs Kongesoger, Jubileumsutgåva 1979, vol. 2, Oslo: Det Norske Samlaget.

Nyberg, Tore (1984), "Stad, skrift och stift", in *Adam av Bremen, historien om Hamburgstiftet och dess biskopar,* Stockholm: Proprius Förlag.

Nyberg, Tore (1997), "Olavskulten i Danmark under medeltiden", in Lars Rumar (ed.), *Helgonet i Nidaros, Olavskult och Kristnande i Norden.*

Storm, Gustav (1880), *Monumenta Historica Norvegica.* Kristiania (Oslo): Brøgger.

Vandvik, Eirik (1959), *Latinske dokument til norsk historie,* Oslo: Det norske samlaget.

Musical Source Material for a Study of the Medieval Use of Nidaros

Owain Tudor Edwards

An Interim Report on an Attempt to Account for the Origin of the Chants in the Liturgy of Nidaros[1]

Spiritual leaders showed determination to have control of the miscellaneous elements which were involved in the performance of religious services from early in the history of the church. By the eleventh century little was left to chance or to the whim of a priest, and detailed regulations were laid down on how services of various kinds were to be conducted. Instructions were given as to the vestments to be worn by the ministering priest, and the choice of texts to be read and the chants to be sung was carefully organised. The provision of such regulations and many more was a prudent attempt to ensure that services would be carried out correctly and with dignity in a period when many of the clergy had little education.

The orders of service for all forms of public, corporate worship officially organised and led by ministers of the church in the middle ages constituted the so-called liturgy.[2] This did not include private forms of Christian devotion. The liturgy's main purpose was to give details for the performance of the mass and the services of the divine office. Finding the full details of the content of these services, and instructions for how these were to be carried out, necessitates referring to all the different kinds of service book in use at a particular time. The comprehensive nature of the task of co-ordinating this information is facilitated by the fact that instructions summarising what had been ordained, normally by an archbishop or bishop, about the content and performance of the liturgy were

---

1 Part of this material was presented at the International Musicological Society meeting at Sopron in 1995 and will appear as "Searching for the music of the use of Nidaros" in *Cantus planus*, (Budapest, forthcoming).
2 Dix, Gregory, *The Shape of the Liturgy* (London 1945), states in the introduction that although "liturgy" refers to all of the official, corporate services it denotes particularly the Eucharist; Davies, J. G. (ed.), *A Dictionary of Liturgy & Worship* (London 1972), p. 222.

also collated and written in an *ordinal*.³ The sum of the information gathered constitutes the *use* followed in a particular church. Generally, although there were exceptions, attempts were made to see that all the parish churches in a diocese, or the religious communities of a particular order, followed the same use. Whether they did so in medieval Nidaros is one of the questions addressed in this essay, in which I shall be dealing with matters concerning the music appointed to be sung in services held in the geographical area of the ecclesiastical province of Nidaros. The metropolitan of the province was the archbishop who had his seat in the city now known as Trondheim.

Few scholars have as yet worked on Norwegian sources of medieval liturgical music and correspondingly little has been published. Georg Reiss wrote an account of the music of the Office of St Olav⁴ which was published in 1912, and Erik Eggen's presentation of the Nidaros sequences was published in 1968.⁵ In addition to these, two theses for masters degrees have been accepted, both by the University of Oslo.⁶ A handful of publications have appeared besides these which are the only substantial studies.⁷ Fortunately, the liturgical content of the material has been examined by Dr Lilli Gjerløw, a medievalist of distinction, whose publication of the *Ordo nidrosiensis ecclesiae* (Oslo 1968) and the *Antiphonarium nidrosiensis ecclesiae* (Oslo 1979) leave all who follow in her debt. The *ordo* is a diplomatic edition of the Nidaros ordinal from surviving sources, while in the second book Dr Gjerløw presents the texts (only) of the antiphonal based on Norwegian sources and relates these to a number of English and Continental uses.

My aim is to describe research being carried out at present by Gisela Attinger, a research fellow at the University of Oslo, and myself to locate what remains, with one important exception, of the musical sources for the medieval use of Nidaros, and to account for its origin. We have, in other words, a typical, "Find, and comment upon" project. Implicit in the aim is a conviction that most of the liturgical music performed in the churches in the ecclesiastical province

---

3   Hughes, Andrew, *Medieval Manuscripts for Mass and Office: a Guide to their Organisation and Terminology* (Toronto 1982).
4   Reiss, Georg, *Musiken ved den middelalderlige Olavsdyrkelse i Norden* (Kristiania 1912).
5   Eggen, Erik, *The Sequences of the Archbishopric of Nidaros* (Copenhagen 1968).
6   Solhaug, Arne J., *En undersøkelse av Ny Kgl. Saml, 138 4to. Et islandsk graduale-håndskrift fra det 16. århundre* (1971), and Attinger, Gisela, *Offisiet "de susceptione sanguinis"—norske gudstjenester fra middelalderen?* (1993).
7   A select bibliography of medieval church music and liturgy in Nordic countries is given in, Bergsagel, John, "Forskning indenfor gregorianik i Danmark—kilder og forskningsstrategier", in Ledang, Ola Kai, (ed.), *Gregorianikk, billedkunst og liturgi i middelalderen* (Trondheim, 1996), pp. 34–38. This includes R. A. Ottóson's study of the Icelandic Office of St. Thorlac (1959), and Ingrid DeGeer's thesis (Uppsala 1985) which includes remarks on the two-part hymn of St. Magnus of Orkney.

of Nidaros will not have been original. The music of the liturgy, like the texts prescribed, was selected from the great repertoire of texts chanted in the Western Church in the later middle ages. This being so, it may be asked, what makes this question at all interesting? The answer lies in the fact that there is ample evidence to show that local, geographical, and chronological variation existed in both major and minor features of the liturgies practised throughout Europe, and that the search to identify the features which went into the composition of a particular liturgy is both challenging and intriguing. I shall shortly give an account of the background to the use of Nidaros, specifying problems which have to be confronted in the inquiry which we are making, but have first to explain the important exception just mentioned. Material for the liturgical celebration of St Olav, the Norwegian patron saint, is currently being investigated by Eyolf Østrem of Uppsala university. Miss Attinger and I have therefore avoided duplicating work in this area.

It needs to be borne in mind that a far fuller and more varied weekly round of services was held in medieval cathedrals, colleges, monasteries and such institutions than would normally be found today. Particularly in Scandinavian countries where the Lutheran Church is strong, attention tends to be concentrated now on Sunday morning service. In many smaller churches, this is the only service held during the week. There may be support in larger congregations for some weekly services, but there are seldom as many as was normal in the middle ages. Services, in medieval times as at present, were made up of a more or less successful and satisfying assortment of liturgical elements, with prayers, readings, possibly a sermon, and the singing of particular kinds of chants by soloists, choir and congregation being involved. Obviously the manner of performing each of these elements offered room for individuality. It is not unreasonable to assume that at different times and in different places many contrasting styles of performance in singing services also came into being. The music was of paramount importance since, apart from the sermon, everything including passages from the Bible and readings from the lives of saints, and prayers, was chanted. The medieval liturgy consisted of action and movement accompanied, or carried forward, by music. While we may *assume* that there will have been differences in the manner of performing the various chants with regard to tempo, voice production, dynamic range, clarity in enunciating of the words, in the pace and intensity with which items followed each, and in the ability of choirs to keep together, we *know* that there was during the middle ages no single order of service which churches throughout Christendom followed in exactly the same manner, with all the same texts and chants being performed for a particular service on a particular day. Uniformity was to come later, after service books printed on paper had replaced hand-written parchment codices, and when travel and communication between areas hundreds of miles apart had become easier. Considering the difficulties there would have been in enforcing liturgical uniformity, it would have been remarkable if such had existed throughout the Western Church in the middle ages. This is not to say that uniformity was never on the agenda, because it was, later, and it was a matter of concern on a diocesan level from the thirteenth century.[8]

Of liturgical uses in England one gradually gained widespread acceptance, this being of the diocese of Salisbury. It was formulated by or for St Osmund (d. 1099), who was William the Conqueror's Chancellor before he became bishop of Salisbury in the South of England. The reason for the influence which it achieved may be attributed to two things. Firstly, it was very thorough and well thought out. It was highly admired for its detailed regulation of services for a non-monastic church,[9] with instructions for the celebration of all the services throughout the year. Secondly, there was a need for a model for general emulation, since such could not be provided, as might have been expected, by the primate of England's own church. The archbishop of Canterbury's cathedral church was in a Benedictine monastery. The forms of service followed there could not provide the norm for the daily services of the office for a non-monastic church. This was why more and more bishops adopted the well-organised Sarum use,[10] which provided solutions to ordinary liturgical problems which had to be faced with parish-church services. By the fifteenth century dioceses throughout most of England as well as Scotland, Ireland and probably also Wales had adopted "Sarum use." As it had been formulated a century before the use of Nidaros came into being, the possibility that it could have had an influence on the latter clearly needs looking at.

It is relevant to inquire about the nature of the sources that may be consulted for finding out how services were performed in medieval Nidaros. There

---

8   Demonstrated by the mass of legislation collected in Powicke, F. M., and Cheney, C. R., *Councils and Synods with other Documents relating to the English Church A.D. 1205–1313* (Oxford 1964).

9   In 1257 its bishop, Giles of Bridport, declared that, "among the churches of the whole world, the church of Sarum hath shone resplendent, like the sun in his full orb, in respect of its divine service, and its ministers". Powicke & Cheney, p. 552, § 2 for the Latin text; the English translation is from Wordsworth, Christopher, *Ceremonies and Processions of the Cathedral Church of Salisbury* (Cambridge 1901), Preface p. vii.

10 A guide to the extensive literature on the Sarum rite is given in Sadie, Stanley, (ed.) *The new Grove's dictionary of music and musicians,* (London 1980), article by Berry, Mary, "Sarum rite", the central work being Frere, W. H., (ed.) *The Use of Sarum* (Cambridge 1898, 1901). Representative sources were also published in facsimile edited by Frere, the *Graduale sarisburiense* (London 1894), and the *Antiphonale sarisburiense* (London 1901–24).

are various kinds: first there are church buildings, defining the physical limits of the liturgical action. Deciding whether a building was dark or light may be relevant in so far as if the church was a very dark one, this might have had an influence of the pace of the proceedings. It would naturally be of interest to see whether there were any wall paintings, sculptures, noteworthy furniture or other forms of functional and visual art adorning the inside of the sacred space which might have a local connection. It would be pertinent to notice whether light entered the church through plain or stained-glass windows, and if the latter were the case, whether the motives depicted were germane to the particular area or the diocese.

Evidence of an organ having been there in medieval times would also be of interest, as an indication at least of the support of a wealthy donor and of a higher-than-average ambition with regard to the performance of the liturgy, because such instruments were not commonplace even in the later middle ages.[11] Distances in the church may be measured as well, in order to get an idea of how long it would take a procession to move from the sacristy to the quire, a matter which would clearly have had an influence on the amount of chant required to be sung during the procession. Then, if the building has not fallen into ruin, it might be possible to raise one's speaking voice or to sing to test the acoustics, to see if the building had a long or a short reverberation time, a matter which again could—but not necessarily—have had a bearing on the rate at which texts might most successfully be intoned in liturgical performance.

An assortment of liturgical vestments and ecclesiastical paraphernalia has survived. These are always valuable objects of study as artefacts surviving from a distant period of time, and of course there are some service books. Despite having these sources for the content of the liturgy, very many questions are left unanswered about how services were carried out because much was taken for granted. Even if books containing all the texts and chants can be found, the manner in which the separate items were performed, say, six hundred years ago, is only hinted at in the written sources.[12]

Episcopal statutes and other ordinances laying down that the relevant books had to be available to officiating priests began to appear generally from the

---

11 Kolnes, Stein Johannes, *Norsk orgelkultur, Instrument og Miljø frå Mellomalderen til i dag* (Oslo 1987), pp. 9–18; Williams, Peter, *A New History of the Organ from the Greeks to the Present Day* (London 1980), chap. 5 "The medieval church organ", pp. 46–54; *Kulturhistorisk Leksikon for Nordisk Middelalder*, (Copenhagen 1956–78), vol. 12, pp. 692–97.
12 For an approach to reconstructing medieval services in performance see the present author's, "Dynamic qualities in the medieval office" in Lillie, Eva Louise, & Petersen, Nils Holger, (eds.), *Liturgy and the Arts in the Middle Ages*, (Copenhagen 1996), pp. 36–63.

early eleventh century. In 1006 or thereabouts the English Archbishop Ælfric decreed, for example, that "every mass-priest should have a mass-book and epistlebook and song-book and reading-book and psalter and handbook and penitential and kalendar".[13] Liturgical material previously available in several books specifically intended for particular users began to be collected in single books in the 11th and 12th centuries. The prayers of the mass, from the sacramentary, the readings, from the lectionary, and the sung items from the cantatorium were increasingly presented together in the *missal*. The *breviary* was compiled from a number of different books of texts, and the musical items for mass and office were correspondingly organised.[14] The *gradual* contained the music of the mass, and the *antiphonary*, or *antiphonal*, the chants with some of the texts for the office.

When considering the origin of the music of the Nidaros liturgy we have to take account of various possibilities with regard to the period of time when Christianity reached the countries which belonged to the province of Nidaros. Influences from the Continent and from what are now known as the British Isles and Ireland could have had an effect on Scandinavian liturgies. The whole of Scandinavia was theoretically part of the archbishopric of Hamburg, although when the archbishopric was erected in 831 most Scandinavians were still heathens. The archbishop's seat was moved to Bremen to escape attack after Hamburg had been sacked by the Vikings in the year 845. Missionaries, with St Ansgar in the lead then attempted to convert Denmark and Sweden, and it is not unreasonable to suppose that there will have been some communication between converts to Christianity in these countries with inhabitants of Norway. But how and when people in the countries which eventually became part of the province of Nidaros adopted the Christian faith are questions that tend to resist precise answers.

The process of converting the inhabitants of Norway and its allied territories to Christianity is thought to have been a gradual one. Brute force and cruelty no doubt characterised the behaviour of many of the Vikings, but the Vikings were also traders and it was in their interest to maintain a workable relationship with their trading partners in the British Isles and on the Continent. It is possible that some of the women captured and brought home to Norway as

---

13 Rankin, Susan, "From memory to record: musical notations in manuscripts from Exeter," *Anglo-Saxon England,* vol. 13 (1984), pp. 97–112, states that there are fragments from over a hundred manuscripts of "songbooks" connected with major ecclesiastical centres like Worcester, Exeter, Sherborne, Canterbury, Durham and Winchester, which contain Anglo-Saxon musical notation, dating from the late tenth and the eleventh centuries.
14 Hughes, p. 118–123.

slaves in the ninth century were Christians, and it is also possible that some Norwegian Vikings chose Christian wives, as we know some of the Vikings who settled in Ireland did in the tenth century. A form of infiltration can have taken place with mothers bringing up their children to their own faith. Speculation along this line of thought lacks proof, however, since slaves and lower-class women did not leave identifiable confirmation of their existence at this time. Nevertheless, on the basis of archaeological evidence found in burial places, it has been suggested that the process of conversion continued over a period as long as a couple of hundred years,[15] culminating in the tenth century in the attempts to convert Norway to Christianity by the three so-called missionary kings, Håkon Adelsteinsfostre, or Håkon the Good (who reigned 945–960); Olav Tryggvason (reigned 995–1000), and Olav Haraldsson, who became St Olav (reigned 1015–1028).

It may perhaps be surprising, in the context of the conference held in Trondheim in July 1997 which focused in particular on the Norwegian patron saint, to recall that Olav Haraldsson had once been a rough and ferocious young man.[16] He participated in Viking raids on England, including one when London bridge was torn down. Having converted to Christianity he brought priests with him from England when he came back to Norway in 1015. These included bishops Sigurd, Grimkjell, Bjarnvard and Rodulv. He met such strong opposition that in 1028 there was little he could do but go into exile. He returned two years later but with an inadequate army not up to the task, and was killed on Wednesday, 29 July 1030, at the Battle of Stiklestad. He was only thirty-five years of age. As he was killed fighting for his faith, he came in a matter of five years to be recognised as a martyr by the people who had rejected his attempt to preach Christianity. His eleven-year old son Magnus was eventually put on the throne and the reputation which grew for the sanctity of the martyr king contributed to ensuring that Christianity had a permanent position in Norway.

When authorities in the Vatican assumed that the people had been converted, Norway was formally included in the ecclesiastical province of Bremen.

---

15 Birkeli, Fridtjov, *Norske steinkors i tidlig middelalder* (Oslo 1973), pp. 8–10, 21; Solli, Brit, "Fra hedendom til kristendom. Religionsskiftet i Norge i arkeologisk belysning", *Viking, Tidsskrift for norrøn arkeologi* vol. 58 (1995), pp. 23–48; Mikkelsen, Egil, "Arabisk sølv og Nordens guder. Islam i vikingfunn", Rindal, Magnus, (ed.) *Fra hedendom til kristendom, perspektiver på religionsskiftet i Norge.* (Oslo 1996), pp. 41–42; Hommedal, Alf Tore, "Frå heller til pilegrimskyrkje. Heilagstaden på Selja", Rindal, Magnus, (ed.) *Fra hedendom til kristendom, perspektiver på religionsskiftet i Norge.* (Oslo 1996), p. 119.

16 See Iversen, Gunilla, "Transforming a Viking into a Saint: The Divine Office of St. Olav" in Baltzer, Rebecca A. & Fassler, Margot M.(eds.), *The Divine Office in the Latin Middles Ages: Methodology and Source Studies, Regional Developments, Hagiography.* (Oxford 1998).

This was in c. 1043, and shortly before 1100 three Norwegian bishoprics were founded: at Nidaros on the estuary, or "os", of the river Nidar (*cf.* the English river "Great Ouse"); further south on the west coast at Selja (the seat of the bishopric was moved to Bjørgvin, or Bergen as the city is now known, in 1170), and the third bishopric was established at the town known variously as Ósló, Ásló and Óslóarherað.[17] The choice of locations has been explained by the connection these places had with the three leading Norwegian saints Olav, Sunniva, and Halvard, respectively. The three bishoprics were assigned one to each of the three great Law-things: Nidaros for the Frostathing, Selje–Bergen for the Gulathing and Oslo for the Eidsivathing.[18] After a few years, in about 1125 the bishopric of Stavanger was separated off from Selja.

Ecclesiastical politics then played an important part. The metropolitan archbishop of Hamburg–Bremen had become one of the most powerful people north of the Alps by the end of the eleventh century. Either in order to reduce his authority, or as part of a general tightening up on diocesan administration, Pope Paschalis II, in agreement with the kings of Denmark, Sweden and Norway,[19] divided this large archbishopric and erected an archbishopric for Scandinavia at Lund in Denmark in 1103. Only a couple of generations later, in 1152 or 53, a new archbishopric with its seat at Nidaros was separated off following a visit by the papal legate, Cardinal Nicolas Breakespear, later known as Pope Adrian IV.[20] A bishopric was founded at Hamar,[21] which with the other mainland bishoprics and six bishoprics in the Norwegian-controlled territories now known as Iceland, Greenland, the Faeroe Isles, the Orkneys, and the Western Isles of Scotland, comprised the province of Nidaros.[22] (Plate 1)

---

17 Nedkvitne, Arne, & Norseng, Per G., *Oslo bys historie* (Oslo 1991), vol. 1, p. 23.
18 Hohler, Christopher, "The Cathedral of St. Swithun at Stavanger in the Twelfth Century," *The Journal of the British Archaeological Association* (Third Series vol. 27, London 1964), p. 94.
19 Ottosen, Knud, *A Short History of the Church of Scandinavia* (Århus 1986), p. 16. In 1133 the archbishop of Hamburg-Bremen's authority over the Nordic countries was temporarily reinstated after an energetic struggle but only for a couple of years: Kolsrud, Oluf, *Noregs kyrkjesoga, I. Millomalderen* (Oslo 1958), p. 181.
20 The same period also saw widespread reorganisation in the Church elsewhere: four archbishops were consecrated in Ireland in 1151 and by 1200, in addition to Denmark and Sweden, Bohemia and Poland had their own archbishoprics. (Davies, J., *A history of Wales,* Harmondsworth 1993, p. 122.)
21 Hohler, *Idem*, observes that the reason behind the foundation of a see at Stavanger which had neither a native patron (Swithun had been bishop of Winchester in England) nor was assigned to a distinct Law-thing, being in the territory of the Gulathing, was a mystery.
22 Lange, Chr. A. & Unger, Carl R., (eds.) *Diplomatarium norvegicum,* (Christiania 1855), vol. 3, pp. 3–6, for Innocent IV's papal bull of 25 February 1253 confirming his predecessor's ruling on the Nidaros bishoprics.

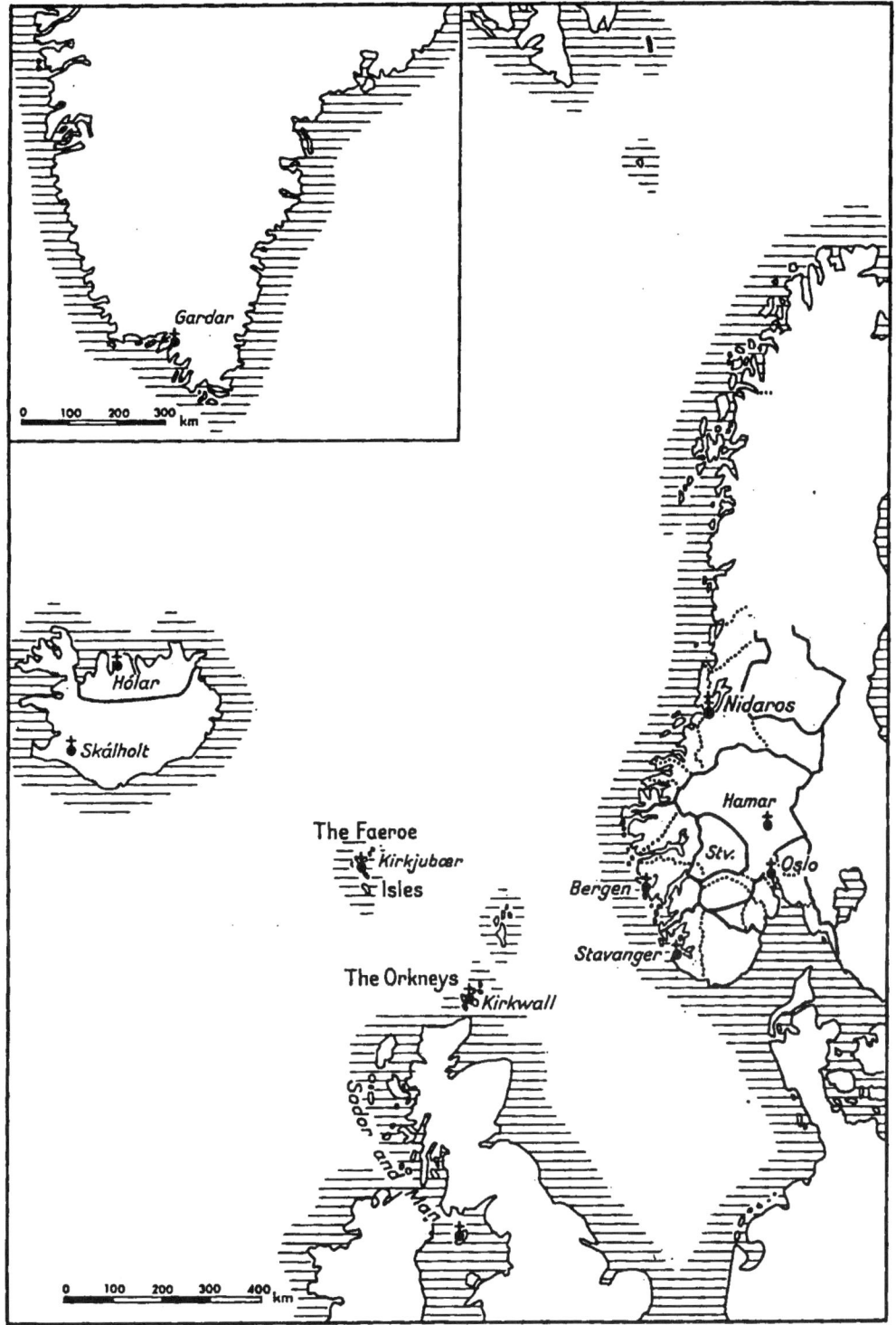

Plate 1. The ecclesiastical province of Nidaros in 1152/3 (from Lilli Gjerløw, *Ordo Nidrosiensis Ecclesiae* (Oslo 1968)

Initially Iceland and Greenland were Norse Viking settlements whose inhabitants were independent, but they submitted to the sovereignty of the Norwegian king in 1262–64 (Iceland) and 1261 (Greenland). However, Norwegian authority over what is now Scotland declined at about the same time. The Hebrides, with the Isle of Man, were ceded to Scotland by the Treaty of Perth in 1266 although they continued to have ecclesiastical allegiance to Nidaros until the fifteenth century, when Man was included in the archbishopric of York (before being transferred to Canterbury in the sixteenth century). Orkney and the Shetland Islands became part of the Scottish kingdom in 1468 and 1469 respectively,[23] and when the archbishopric of St. Andrews was erected four years later, they were formally incorporated in its province.[24]

Although far flung, the component parts of the province of Nidaros were bound together by the ocean. This was not without its perils, but communication by sea was in reasonable weather often easier than travel overland in the middle ages and the Vikings were, as is well documented, accomplished mariners. Bearing this in mind, the Western Isles of Scotland, and Greenland, for example, do not appear as peripheral or as distant and inaccessible from Nidaros. The settlements on coast and island were connected by sea routes. The amount of traffic to Greenland or the Faeroe islands might have been relatively small, while westward to the Scottish Isles and Ireland it was probably not inconsiderable.

Despite its geographical extent, the province was relatively poor. The task of meeting the expenditure of building churches and providing the necessary church vestments, ornaments and books will have been a severe test of belief in their new religion, particularly for the inhabitants who had but recently been forcibly converted[25] and, from the twelfth century, forced to pay tithes.[26]

Seen in this light, the erection of the magnificent cathedral at Nidaros with the archbishop's palace right next to it was an extraordinary achievement. A factor which contributed to the possibility of being able to pay for the building work was the appeal which the shrine of St Olav exerted as a centre of pilgrimage,

---

23 The political reasons for the transfer are discussed in Nicholson, Ranald, *Scotland: The Later Middle Ages. The Edinburgh History of Scotland vol. 1* (Edinburgh 1974), pp. 82, 413–19.

24 Fryde, E.B., Greenway, D. E., Porter, S., & Roy, I., *Handbook of British Chronology* (London 1986), pp. 300, 314.

25 The most comprehensive account of the financial state of the province of Nidaros, albeit of a later period, may be seen in Storm, Gustav, *Afgifter fra den Norske Kirkeprovins til det Apostoliske Kammer og Kardinalkollegiet 1311–1523 efter Optegnelser i de Pavelige Arkiver* (Christiania 1897).

26 Introduced systematically in the twelfth century in the reign of King Sigurd Jorsalfare (reigned 1123–30) to provide the Church with a secure economic foundation. (Fladeby, Rolf, Imsen, Steinar & Winge, Harald, (eds.), *Norsk Historisk Leksikon* (Oslo 1981), p. 342; Kortner, Olaf, Munthe, Preben & Tveterås, Egil, (eds.), *Aschehoug og Gyldendals Store Norske Leksikon* (Oslo 1986–89), vol. 12, p. 225.

and consequently the repository of the offerings of the *peregrini*.[27] From early in the history of the Church a desire to visit the lands of the Bible, and the wish to venerate the graves of the martyrs elsewhere in Europe, had played a significant part in the minds of devout Christians.[28] Attending the places mentioned in the Bible was a means of verifying the Scriptures, and early pilgrims' accounts show how people were avidly interested in seeing the places they had heard about. The description written by the pilgrim Egeria of her journey to the Holy Land in about 381–84, for example, shows this very well and provides valuable information about the early liturgy.[29] But more important than travel motivated primarily by devotional interest, was the concept of pilgrimage as *penance*.

This originated in Ireland between the sixth and the eighth centuries, and developed into a conventional scale of penalties which a priest could impose for atonement of sins confessed.[30] The price of obtaining absolution was graduated appropriately with the seriousness of the misdemeanours for which the penitent sought forgiveness. Penance for serious sins might include long periods of fasting or even exile, but for practical reasons this system fell into disuse. It was replaced by other forms of redemption for sins committed. For rich people these could include contributions to the church in the form of gifts of land, for instance, or through an endowment to a particular church or monastery.

There was a scriptural basis to the practice which was seen as a valuable act of piety, since that of discretely giving alms had been encouraged by Our Lord. Matthew 6, 3–4[31]: *when you do some act of charity, do not let your left hand know what your right is doing; your good deed must be secret, and your Father who sees what is done in secret will reward you.* In the Old Testament almsgiving was enjoined more explicitly, in the form of covenant, Tobit iv, 9–10: *you will be laying up a sound insurance against the day of adversity. Almsgiving saves the giver from death and keeps him from going down into darkness,* and in the middle ages "almsgiving" acquired a broader meaning for contrite penitents of the well-endowed kind.

People who could not afford to be very generous to the church might, nevertheless, chose to take advantage of papal indulgences when these were available. These were a means of atonement that to some extent replaced earlier forms of penance. Indulgences, of the kind to which penitential exercise were

---

27 Nilsson, Bertil, (ed.) *Kristnandet i Sverige. Gamla källor och nya perspektiv* (Uppsala 1996), p. 395.
28 Which may be compared with the Islamic tradition by which Moslems visit holy places in Saudi Arabia.
29 Schjøth, Else (trans.) & Dahl, Ellert (Introduction) *Egerias reise til Det Hellige Land* (Oslo 1991).
30 Hohler, Christopher, "The badge of St. James", *The Scallop* (London 1957), pp. 52–54.
31 Quotations from *The New English Bible* (Oxford 1970).

attached became popular, and pilgrimage to Rome had by the ninth century become a form of penance required for grave offences. After Jerusalem and Rome, the grave of St James the apostle at Santiago de Compostela in north-western Spain had by the eleventh century become the third pilgrimage of Christendom.[32] By the early thirteenth century the idea of pilgrimage had become generalised to include other sanctuaries, and particular places in every country gained attention as the goals upon which sincere religious adherents and contrite penitents alike set their sights. Reasons for embarking upon pilgrimages are numerous and by no means all pilgrims were making redress for sins committed. Journeys might be made in the belief that illness or disability which the pilgrim had, or which another person represented had, would be cured as a result of praying at the relics of a particular saint. Miracles inevitably embellished and became entwined with travellers tales and these contributed to nurturing the cult of the saint in question. In Scandinavia, Nidaros seems to have had a magnetic attraction for people committing themselves to attenuated periods of meditation, while undergoing the discomforts and hazards of a long walk to the shrine of Norway's *rex perpetuus,* St Olav, for the remission of sin.[33]

The offerings of the pilgrims added to the income of Nidaros and the cathedral chapter also gradually increased in size. The number of canons rose from fifteen in 1253 to twenty by the end of the middle ages.[34] Comparable religious foundations elsewhere were sometimes more richly endowed. Norman cathedral chapters had between twenty-five and fifty canons, while Chatres had seventy-seven at the beginning of the fourteenth century.[35] The chapter of Lincoln in England, whose cathedral architecturally was the main source of inspiration for the builders of Nidaros, had fifty-four canons. So had Wells. Salisbury had fifty-two, York thirty-six, St Paul's in London had thirty major and twelve

---

32 Hohler, (1957), p. 54.

33 Gjerløw, Lilli, (ed.), *Ordo nidrosiensis ecclesiae* (Oslo 1968), p. 126, refers to an indulgence "*de remissione*" by Pope Alexander III and to the *innumera populorum confluentia*, the innumerable people pouring into Nidaros. There is an extensive literature on this subject from which the following selection give both reasons for embarking upon a pilgrimage and something of the atmosphere of strenuous devotion necessary to carry it out. Hall, D. J., *English mediaeval pilgrimage* (London 1965); Sumption, Jonathan, *Pilgrimage, an image of mediaeval religion* (London 1975); Brooke, Rosalind and Christopher, *Popular Religion in the Middle Ages* (London 1984); Krötzl, Christian, *Pilger, Mirakel und Alltag, Formen des Verhaltens im skandinavischen Mittelalter* (Helsinki 1994); Nygård, Mette, — *Og vegjine falle så vide—Om gamle og nye pilgrimsmål* (Oslo 1996). The popularity in England of Canterbury cathedral with its shrine of St Thomas was immortalised in Geoffrey Chaucer's well-known *Canterbury Tales.*

34 Kolsrud, Oluf, "Korsongen I Nidarosdomen", *Festskrift til O. M. Sandvik 70-års dagen* (Oslo 1945), p. 97.

35 Edwards, Kathleen, *The English Secular Cathedrals in the Middle Ages* (Manchester 1949), p. 33. Kolsrud (1945) gives details of the number of canons in other Scandinavian cathedral chapters pp. 97–103.

minor canons, Chichester and Hereford had twenty-eight canons, Exeter had twenty-four, Lichfield twenty-one.

The cathedral churches of the suffragan bishops of Nidaros were not as well endowed, and it has been pointed out by Oluf Kolsrud, who examined records of ecclesiastical appointments in the province, that while there were chapters of twelve canons in Bjørgvin and Oslo, the number was less at Stavanger and Hamar. The chapters created for the bishoprics of the Orkneys (with seat at Kirkwall), and the Hebrides and Man have an uncertain history, but it is known that there were never chapters of canons at Hólar and Skálholt in Iceland, nor in the Faeroe Isles nor Greenland. Icelandic bishops were chosen by the priests and the people; the bishop of the Faeroes was elected at Bjørgvin, and bishops of Greenland were elected at Nidaros.[36]

The canons were priests from whose number the senior dignitaries who had responsibility for the daily running of the cathedral services were chosen. Apart from the dignitaries whose duties compelled them to reside permanently close to the cathedral, the canons also had care of parish churches out in the country, but they took turns at serving in the cathedral for a few months at a time, leaving a deputy[37] to take services in the parish church. The responsibility for organising the performance of the liturgy in each of the larger cathedrals, which in the middle ages was synonymous with leading the choir in the music and singing certain solo parts himself, had to be undertaken by a man of musical ability. On the Continent and in England the precentor was one of the four dignitaries of the cathedral (along with the dean, treasurer and chancellor). This convention may not have been followed in the province of Nidaros, for documentation has not been found showing that precentorships existed before the 1490s at Nidaros, Bjørgvin, Oslo, or Hamar.[38] Evidence is lacking as to when cathedral choirs were established in the province, but there is no reason to assume that choirs did not exist, consisting of full-time professional singers, nor that boys from the cathedral school will not also have sung on certain occasions.[39]

---

36 Kolsrud (1958), p. 192.
37 Latin, *vicarius*, hence "the Vicar" which is still how many parish priests in the Church of England are referred to today.
38 Kolsrud, p. 365 says before 1500. I am indebted to Audun Dybdahl for drawing my attention to evidence of a contract for sale of land in 1494 to the bishop of Oslo which was witnessed by Narwe Thoresson, *cantor*, (Ms. Dipl. Arn. Magn. fasc. 96 no. 6).
39 For the most comprehensive history of the schools attached to the Norwegian cathedrals and monasteries in the middle ages see: Øverås, Asbjørn, Erichsen, A. E., & Due, Johan, *Trondheim Katedralskoles Historie 1152–1952* (Trondheim 1952), pp. 13–67; Høigård, Einar & Ruge, Herman, *Den Norske Skoles Historie* (Oslo 1963), pp. 15–20; Ording, Fr. & Boyesen, Einar, *Pedagogikkens Historie* (Oslo 1968), pp. 214–17.

Nidaros was an integral part of the Western Church where similar conventions applied as elsewhere, from Rome to Paris, or Cologne to Canterbury, and services were sung not only in cathedrals, but also in monasteries where the number of monks permitted it, and in larger parish churches as well. The number of canons who were present in Nidaros in 1253 when the papal bull of Innocent IV confirming details of the extent of the province was read was fifteen.[40] This would have been the number in residence at the time not the total number of canons. In 1554 the number would appear to have been twenty.[41]

With regard to the question of whether the choirs also included boys, the anecdote about the seven-year-old Håkon Håkonsson who had started as a pupil at the cathedral school at Nidaros might be borne in mind. When asked by Earl Håkon his father in 1211 what he learned there he replied, "Singing, my Lord," to which his father replied that he did not need to learn to sing since he was not going to become a priest.[42] In England, in non-monastic cathedrals like Nidaros, each canon was expected to employ a "vicar-choral" to sing full time for him in the cathedral choir even when he was in residence.[43] It is particularly regrettable that Nidaros cathedral was almost destroyed by fire on five occasions, in 1328, 1432, 1531, 1708 and 1719. The original choir stalls which could have given an indication of the size of the choir, and which would have confirmed that the cathedral choir sat as was conventional with the stalls in three tiers facing each other on either side of the aisle, have consequently long since disappeared.

It took some time before the selection of liturgical material necessary to constitute a new use of Nidaros had been carried out. It is reasonable to assume that the priests initially appointed must have brought books with them. They would have needed these to support their memory of the liturgy until service books providing material for the new use had been compiled. The full range of service books, in reasonably large numbers, must have been imported for utilisation by the clergy in churches in those areas which were eventually included in the archbishopric of Nidaros during the first two hundred and fifty years when Christianity was generally becoming the accepted religion of the people. The process of conversion will have continued through the eleventh and twelfth

---

40 Lange & Unger, vol. 3, p. 6.
41 Dybdahl, Audun, *Jordeiendomsforhold og godseiere i Trøndelag. Fra Aslak Bolt til Landkommisjonen* (Steinkjer 1989), p. 190.
42 Hødnebø, Finn & Magerøy, Hallvard (eds.), *Soga om Håkon Håkonsson, Norges Kongesagaer* (Oslo 1979), vol. 4, p. 30.
43 Harrison, Frank Ll., *Music in Medieval Britain* (London 1958), pp. 4–9; Edwards, Kathleen, pp. 257–91; Robertson, Anne Walters, *The Service-Books of the Royal Abbey of Saint-Denis, Images of Ritual and Music in the Middle Ages* (Oxford 1991), pp. 306, 311–13, and 317.

centuries. The *Ordo nidrosiensis ecclesiae* dates from the early thirteenth century, and was probably completed under the supervision the third metropolitan of Nidaros, Archbishop Eirik Ivarsson (1189–1205).[44]

The compilers of the ordinal had a choice between two main liturgical traditions from which to select material. On the Continent to the South was the weight of German influence, while the liturgical traditions of England and France existed in the West. German uses not unexpectedly influenced uses in the adjoining countries Denmark and Sweden where St Ansgar, the "Apostle of the North", had been active.[45] French and English liturgical traditions had many characteristics which might be emulated. Inevitably in a period when the Norman-French conquerors dominated England, the English liturgies witness to French influence. More specifically, English liturgical practice and ecclesiastical organisation were subject to *fundamental reform* after the Norman Conquest. Presumably the selection of material for the Nidaros ordinal was affected by the personal preferences of Archbishop Eirik Ivarsson. Because of conflict with the king he moved to Denmark in 1190 where for twelve years his experience of the daily liturgy was at the former metropolitan cathedral of Scandinavia at Lund. He remained there until King Sverre's death in 1202. It is not known how much of the work on the ordinal had been done by his predecessor, the second metropolitan, Øystein Erlendsson (1161–88), but conflict with the king had also forced him into exile, and he lived in England for three years (1180–83).

By the beginning of the fourteenth century the Church had developed into a powerful institution and it has been estimated that there were in the region of 1300 churches and 28 monasteries in Norway before successive onslaughts of bubonic plague beginning in 1349, 1359 and 1370 reduced the population drastically.[46] If the practice in Nidaros was similar to that of England, all of these institutions will have had to have acquired the necessary liturgical books.[47] During the first four centuries after Christianity had been introduced in Norway,

---

44 In *Ordo nidrosiensis ecclesiae* (Oslo 1968), p. 30, Dr Gjerløw points out that Archbishop Eirik is referred to in the text as dominus, while the previous archbishop, Øystein, is referred to as of *bone memorie*, and *venerande memorie*. Eirik, however, having lost his sight, resigned in 1205 but did not die until 1213. For a biography of the second archbishop see Gunnes, Erik, *Erkebiskop Øystein* (Oslo 1996).
45 Helander, Sven, *Ansgarskulten i norden* (Stockholm 1989). The saint was not celebrated in the Nidaros liturgy.
46 *Aschehougs Konversasjonsleksikon* (Oslo 1974), vol. 14, p. 612.
47 Aspects of the question of how many liturgical books would have been in use in the late middle ages in Great Britain are discussed in the present author's article, "How many Sarum antiphonals were there in England and Wales in the middle of the sixteenth century?" *Revue Bénédictine*, vol. 99 (1989), pp. 155–80.

all of these will have been hand-written on vellum or parchment. Printed editions of the Nidaros missal and the breviary were not published until 1519,[48] only eighteen years before the Reformation.

At the beginning of this essay I stated that it was an interim report on an attempt to account for the origin of the chants found in material representing the use of Nidaros. The aim is to examine the music of the liturgy for services as prescribed in the Nidaros ordinal. Basically, this means finding books exemplifying early and late stages of Nidaros use from each of the sees, making a selection and then systematically comparing the position and exact form of each chant with Scandinavian, Continental and British sources representing other uses. The strongest liturgical influence on the choice of Nidaros texts, Lilli Gjerløw has shown, was that of Norman-English liturgical practice. It ought to have been a fairly easy task to find confirmation of this in the variants of the chants used. It has not proved to be quite that straight forward, however, because Latin service books of medieval Nidaros use are unusually scarce. In fact, the greatest difficulty which we have at present is finding enough source material.

Most of the remaining medieval liturgical material has been deposited in the National Archives of Norway (Riksarkivet, which is in Oslo). Small collections are in regional state archives and university libraries. The material is almost all of a fragmentary nature, consisting of incomplete books, odd leaves and, most frequently, small fragments. The origin of the material is, moreover, difficult to determine, so it is frequently impossible to say categorically that a fragment represents the use of Nidaros. Many of the fragments are so small in size that they do not contain enough material to be able to confirm the fact that the sequence of items agrees with the items specified in the ordinal.

A fragment may be said to have originated in a service book which was used in the province of Nidaros, but such a book was quite probably imported and could represent any number of uses, secular or monastic. The Latin service books collected in after the Reformation (1537) were kept in the chanceries of the royal administrators. One of the functions which officials at these chanceries had was to record the value of lands for taxation purposes. Towards the end of the sixteenth century someone came upon the idea that the old books could be put to some use: leaves of vellum made good folders for documents. When cut up into strips the material could also be utilised for securing quires of land-assessment accounts together. The vellum or parchment was stiffer than the soft paper on which accounts were written, so quires of paper were sewn through each

---

48 *Missale Nidrosiense* (Copenhagen 1519), *Breviarium Nidrosiense* (Paris 1519).

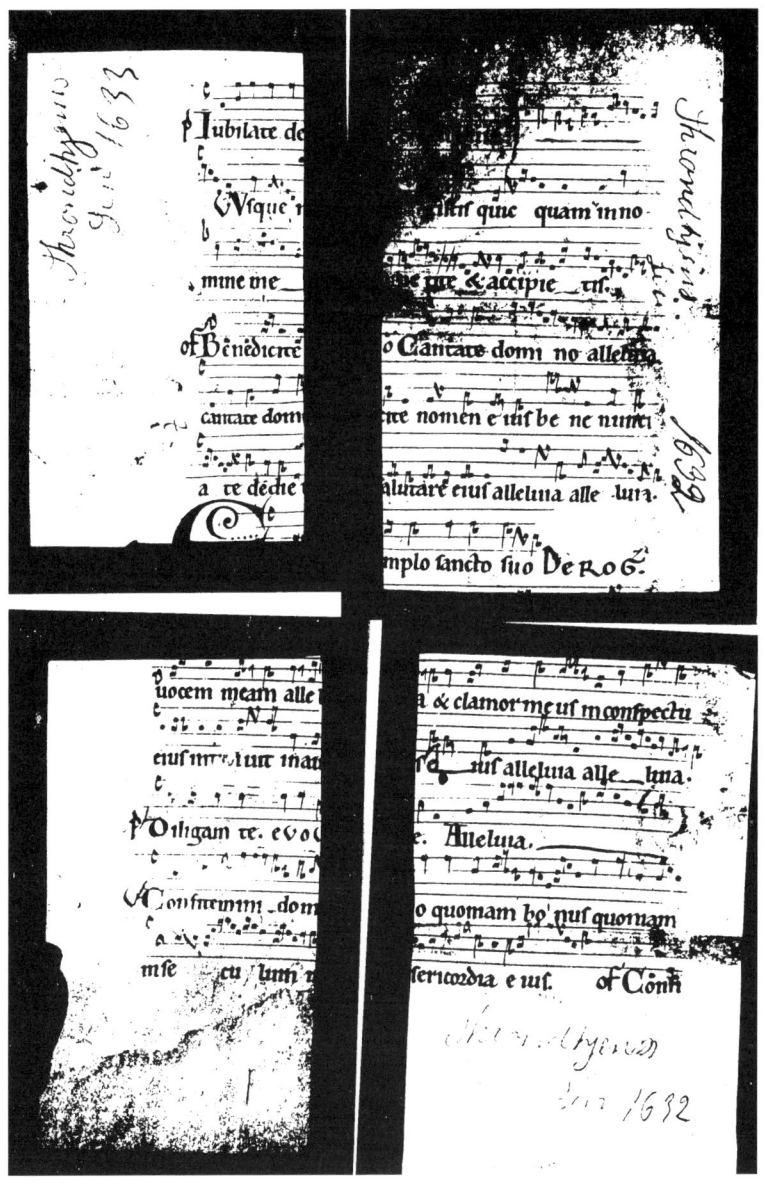

Plate 2. Fragments with annotation Throndhjems Len 1632/33. By kind permission of the National Archives of Norway.

with a piece of vellum on the spine. These pieces of binding material vary considerably in size, but most of them are smaller than the palm of a hand (Plate 2).

Some of the fragments bear legible inscriptions giving the chancery district concerned and the year of the evaluation of property for taxation purposes. It is unlikely that books were carried far before being torn asunder for binding purposes, although this could obviously have happened. It has been assumed, therefore, that the liturgical vellum or parchment was put to use in the chancery of the district closest to where the books had been used in church. Following this hypothesis, the bishopric in which the liturgical books were used before their re-utilisation in the seventeenth-century may be deduced. This is as close as it is possible to come to the provenance, unless internal evidence affords additional information. A serious objection exists that must be admitted, namely, that by the late middle ages a trade in the production and sale of books grew up which catered particularly for the ecclesiastical market. We know liturgical books were imported, which means the assumption that manuscripts were drawn exclusively from particular areas has to be viewed with caution, and since some of the fragments in Norwegian archives became separated from the documents to which they were attached in the seventeenth century, the secondary provenance of these was consequently lost as well.

The fragments at the National Archives, amounting probably to no more than five thousand in all, have been sorted into *c*. 1200 envelopes. These contain liturgical texts both with and without the chants, written with musical notation in different palaeographic styles, from pre-Conquest Anglo-French to late medieval Continental and English. There is nowhere approaching enough material to provide evidence for what was sung throughout the whole of the church year. Nor is there enough material to enable a comparison to be made between what might be considered an early (twelfth-century) Nidaros witness and a late one contemporary with the printed breviary and missal.

Medieval liturgical material fortunately survived far better in Iceland than elsewhere in the province of Nidaros and there are as many as four more-or-less complete Icelandic manuscripts of the ordinal (compared with only half a page which survived in Norway). On the other hand, no liturgical books *at all* seem to have survived from Greenland. Difficulty in locating material can arise because the frontiers of the Norwegian mainland have been redrawn since the Reformation. Båhuslen which extended Norwegian territory south-east from the present frontier almost to Gothenburg, for example, was ceded to Sweden in 1658. For two years Sweden also held the county of Trondheim, including Nidaros itself. Norway was integrally associated with both Denmark and Sweden at various times. It was part of the united kingdom of Denmark-Norway from 1381 to 1814 before it became an independent state in union with Sweden under the Swedish king. Complete independence under a Norwegian king was only regained in 1905. Because of its political history, searches for relevant material need to be carried out in the national archives of each of the countries with which "member nations" of medieval Nidaros were involved, not forgetting Greenland and the Faeroes with Denmark, and the Scottish Isles and Man with England.

The most difficult question is deciding what constitutes Nidaros material, because the fact that a manuscript might eventually have ended up being used as a binding in a Norwegian chancery by no means guarantees that it had a Norwegian origin. Judging by the musical palaeography, many of the fragments may be taken to have come from imported books.[49] Palaeographic studies of Norwegian scriptoria have yet to be done, and so categorical statements on the provenance of liturgical fragments are seldom possible. The textual content of the material may only to a certain extent be helpful. We would naturally be on the look out for Nidaros saints like Olav, Halvard (of Oslo), Sunnive (Selje), Magnus (Orkney),and Thorlak (Iceland). They could be named in Kalendars, they might appear in the Litany, or even have special provision in the Sanctorale. A word of warning was given by Dr Gjerlow in her book on the Nidaros antiphonal, about not taking anything for granted, however, since in her experience surviving Nidaros sources were notoriously unfaithful to the ordinal!

We know from her investigation of the material that all the normal kind of services were performed in the province. The ordinal gives details of all the items, and this shows—if such proof were necessary—that practices in Nidaros were in line with those of the rest of the Western Church in the middle ages, notwithstanding its distant and peripheral position in relation to Rome geographically. The intention was much the same throughout Europe, although the manner in which it would have been put into practice will obviously have been very different, because of the resources available, if comparison were made between a well-endowed parish church in Rome and the church in a little village in Norway or Greenland.

The chants in the Nidaros fragments have to be compared with representative Continental and English sources of the same chants. Here in contrast with the paucity of Nidaros sources, is the question of deciding which, and how many, might practically be drawn into the comparison, from a surfeit of riches. This constitutes a strong challenge for systematic classification and interpretation.[50] An impression of the kind and number of melodic details which occur in various readings of the same chant may be obtained from the following exam-

---

49 Gjerløw (1979), *passim*; and Kolsrud, p. 365.
50 Helpful information is provided on manuscripts representing different uses in Hughes, and in Hiley, David, "The Norman chant traditions—Normandy, Britain, Sicily" (*Proceedings of the Royal Musical Association,* vol. 107 (1980–81), and in the same author's comprehensive study, "Ordinary of mass chants in English, North French and Sicilian manuscripts" (*Journal of the Plainsong & Mediæval Music Society*, vol. 9, 1986).

ple, which I have taken from the only surviving page of a psalter in the National Archives. The chant given is the antiphon *Benedictus dominus in eternum*, which was sung with Psalm 88 *Misericordas domini in æternum cantabo* at matins on Friday mornings (*feria vi ad matutinas*).

This is a very short and simple chant which resembles the traditional formula for intoning psalms in the sixth mode. I have compared it with a selection of sources and noted the places where something is different in the other chants (Plate 3). All of these except for London, British Library, MS Addl. 23935, which is a Dominican book, are British. It may be seen that even though this kind of chant is one of the simplest and shortest in the repertory of liturgical chant, there are points where differences occur. The note f on *"in" eternum* in the Norwegian fragment is in agreement with five of the sources with which the chant is compared here but four other sources are different. If reference is made to Dom Jean Claire's survey of Continental sources with variants of all the short Psalter antiphons,[51] it may be seen that the Continental versions which he includes have the note **f** on this syllable. That differences of this kind are present in such a short chant, particularly one which was sung regularly every week, underlines the need to examine all the details with great care to identify the versions having the closest resemblance. This being one of the commonest and most well-known chants would have been learned by every chorister in his student days when he committed the Psalter to memory. Arguably, variant readings arose for this antiphon because it was so frequently sung that it was more susceptible to seeing local ways of performing it gradually taking root. Chants which were only sung once a year, on the other hand, might show melodic differences for the reason that they were not remembered correctly from time to time.

The present survey of the chants used in the use of Nidaros ought to be completed in a few years time. Whether the musical variants of the Nidaros chants generally reflect the German-Danish tradition or the Anglo-French it is not as yet possible to say. As Dr Gjerløw's research indicates that the texts chosen clearly fell under the influence of Norman liturgical reforms, it will be surprising if the strongest influence turned out to come from Germany. The hypothesis which my colleague and I are working on is that the music of the medieval Nidaros liturgy was derived from French and/or Norman-English uses. We continue accumulating evidence that will confirm or disprove it. There is nothing like enough material to provide a valid statistical basis. The number

---

51 Claire, Jean, "Les répertoires liturgiques latins avant l'octoéchos, i, L'Office férial romano-franc", *Études Grégoriennes,* (Solesmes 1975), vol. 15, pp. 5–192.

Oslo, Riksarkivet,
Lat. Fragm. (47) 837.1

Cambridge, University Library, MS Dd. xii. 67	exactly the same			
Hereford, Cathedral, Chapter Library, MS P. 9. vii	exactly the same			
London, British Library, MS Addl. 35285	exactly the same			
London, British Library, MS Addl. 23935	exactly the same			
Aberystwyth, National Library of Wales, MS 20541 E (Temporale)			g	
Cambridge, University Library, MS Mm. ii. 9				⁻° gf
Aberystwyth, National Library of Wales, MS 20541 E (Psalter)			g	⁻° gf
London, British Library, MS Lansdowne 463			g	⁻° gf
Worcester, Cathedral, Chapter Library, MS F. 160		(-c)	fga	⁻° gf

Plate 3. Comparison of *Benedictus* chants. The sign ⁻° indicates a liquescence.

of surviving chants is far less than the total number of chants which are lacking. The provenance of the material which has survived is, as has repeatedly been emphasised, questionable anyway.

When Archbishop Erik Valkendorf carried out a visitation of the province of Nidaros in 1512, he realised that his predecessors had obviously failed to execute the intention of the ordinal to enforce liturgical uniformity. Service books representing many different uses were being employed throughout Nidaros and this was the main reason for his enjoining his subordinates to use the breviary and missal which he had had printed in 1519. Deploring the haphazard use of foreign books in his forward to the breviary, he says he had found congregations using books of Roman use, and service books from Cologne, Lund, Uppsala and Utrecht. There were Sarum books from England and also Cistercian, Franciscan and Dominican service books.[52] Considering that travel in the province of Nidaros could be hazardous by sea and not without difficulty on land either, the situation is not unexpected. Had travel been easier, inspection of the service books could have been carried out by episcopal representatives more frequently, until a higher degree of uniformity had been attained. In view of the fact that so little liturgical material has survived, and that that which remains is chiefly in the form of fragments of manuscripts, we have very good reason to appreciate Archbishop Valkendorf's endeavours which led to the printing of all the liturgical texts. It is unfortunate that the antiphonal and the gradual were not printed as well! The Church throughout Europe had been made to focus attention on service books back in the thirteenth century. Measures were taken following decrees of the Fourth General Council of the Lateran in Rome in 1215, the objects of which were to prepare for a new crusade and to instigate reforms for the universal Church.[53] The enforcement of such measures was more easily achieved in some areas than others, and episcopal statutes show that these were matters of lasting concern right up to the Reformation.

Parish priests in the province of Nidaros were less easily disciplined than many on account of the remoteness of their dwelling places. Considering the assortment of liturgical material which was being used, as shown by the remaining fragments of service books in the National Archives, and as witnessed and commented upon by Archbishop Valkendorf, there are grounds for asserting that the uniformity intended by the Nidaros ordinal was *never* successfully enforced.

---

52 Archbishop Erik Valkendorf's forward to the Nidaros Breviary (1519), p. 4. For a description of the breviary and the missal see Gjerløw, Lilli, "The Breviarium and the Missale Nidrosiense (1519)," *Proceedings of the Seventh International Symposium organized by the Centre for the Study of Vernacular Literature in the Middle Ages: From Script to Book* Bekker-Nielsen, Hans et al. (eds.), (Odense 1983), pp. 50–77, 168–69.
53 Powicke, F. M., & Cheney, C. R., p. 47.

Bibliography

Aschehougs Konversasjonsleksikon (Oslo 1974).

Attinger, Gisela, *Offisiet "de susceptione sanguinis"—norske gudstjenester fra middelalderen?* (1993).

Baltzer, Rebecca A. & Fassler, Margot M.(eds.), *The Divine Office in the Latin Middles Ages: Methodology and Source Studies, Regional Developments, Hagiography* (Oxford 1998).

Bekker-Nielsen, Hans et al. (eds.), *Proceedings of the Seventh International Symposium organized by the Centre for the Study of Vernacular Literature in the Middle Ages: From Script to Book* (Odense 1983).

Bergsagel, John, "Forskning indenfor gregorianik i Danmark—kilder og forskningsstrategier", Ledang, Ola Kai, (ed.), *Gregorianikk, billedkunst og liturgi i middelalderen* (Trondheim, 1996).

Berry, Mary, "Sarum rite", Sadie, Stanley, (ed.) *The new Grove's dictionary of music and musicians* (London 1980).

Birkeli, Fridtjov, *Norske steinkors i tidlig middelalder* (Oslo 1973).

Breviarium nidrosiense (Paris 1519).

Brooke, Rosalind & Christopher, *Popular Religion in the Middle Ages* (London 1984).

Claire, Jean, "Les répertoires liturgiques latins avant l'octoéchos, i, L'Office férial romano-franc", *Études Grégoriennes* (Solesmes 1975).

Davies, J. G. (ed.), *A Dictionary of Liturgy & Worship* (London 1972).

Davies, J., *A history of Wales* (Harmondsworth 1993).

De Geer, I., *Earl, Saint, Bishop, Skald—and Music. The Orkney Earldom of the Twelfth Century. A Musicological Study* (Uppsala 1985).

Dix, Gregory, *The Shape of the Liturgy* (London 1945).

Dybdahl, Audun, *Jordeiendomsforhold og godseiere i Trøndelag. Fra Aslak Bolt til Landkommisjonen* (Steinkjer 1989).

Edwards, Kathleen, *The English Secular Cathedrals in the Middle Ages* (Manchester 1949).

Edwards, Owain Tudor, "How many Sarum antiphonals were there in England and Wales in the middle of the sixteenth century?" *Revue Bénédictine,* vol. 99 (1989).

Edwards, Owain Tudor, "Dynamic qualities in the medieval office", Lillie, Eva Louise, & Petersen, Nils Holger, (eds.), *Liturgy and the Arts in the Middle Ages* (Copenhagen 1996).

Eggen, Erik, *The Sequences of the Archbishopric of Nidaros* (Copenhagen 1968).

Fladby, Rolf, Imsen, Steinar & Winge, Harald, (eds.), *Norsk Historisk Leksikon* (Oslo 1981).

Frere, W. H., (ed.) *Antiphonale sarisburiense* (London 1901–24).

Frere, W. H., (ed.) *Graduale sarisburiense* (London 1894).

Frere, W. H., (ed.) *The Use of Sarum* (Cambridge 1898, 1901).

Fryde, E.B., Greenway, D. E., Porter, S., & Roy, I., *Handbook of British Chronology* (London 1986).

Gjerløw, Lilli, (ed.), *Antiphonarium nidrosiensis ecclesiae* (Oslo 1979).

Gjerløw, Lilli, (ed.), *Ordo nidrosiensis ecclesiae* (Oslo 1968).

Gjerløw, Lilli, "The Breviarium and the Missale Nidrosiense (1519)," Bekker-Nielsen, Hans et al. (eds.), *Proceedings of the Seventh International Symposium organized by the Centre for the Study of Vernacular Literature in the Middle Ages: From Script to Book* (Odense 1983).

Gunnes, Erik, *Erkebiskop Øystein* (Oslo 1996).

Hall, D. J., *English mediaeval pilgrimage* (London 1965).

Harrison, Frank Ll., *Music in Medieval Britain* (London 1958).

Helander, Sven, *Ansgarskulten i norden* (Stockholm 1989).

Hiley, David, "Ordinary of mass chants in English, North French and Sicilian manuscripts", *Journal of the Plainsong & Mediæval Music Society*, vol. 9, 1986.

Hiley, David, "The Norman chant traditions—Normandy, Britain, Sicily", *Proceedings of the Royal Musical Association,* vol. 107 (1980–81).

Hohler, Christopher, "The badge of St. James", *The Scallop* (London 1957).

Hohler, Christopher, "The Cathedral of St. Swithun at Stavanger in the Twelfth Century," *The Journal of the British Archaeological Association* (Third Series vol. 27, London 1964).

Hommedal, Alf Tore, "Frå heller til pilegrimskyrkje. Heilagstaden på Selja", in Rindal, Magnus, (ed.) *Fra hedendom til kristendom, perspektiver på religionsskiftet i Norge* (Oslo 1996).

Hughes, Andrew, *Medieval Manuscripts for Mass and Office: a Guide to their Organisation and Terminology* (Toronto 1982).

Hødnebø, Finn & Magerøy, Hallvard (eds.), *Soga om Håkon Håkonsson, Norges Kongesagaer* (Oslo 1979).

Høigård, Einar & Ruge, Herman, *Den Norske Skoles Historie* (Oslo 1963).

Iversen, Gunilla, "Transforming a Viking into a Saint: The Divine Office of St. Olav", Baltzer, Rebecca A. & Fassler, Margot M.(eds.), *The Divine Office in the Latin Middles Ages: Methodology and Source Studies, Regional Developments, Hagiography* (Oxford 1998).

Kolnes, Stein Johannes, *Norsk orgelkultur, Instrument og Miljø frå Mellomalderen til i dag* (Oslo 1987).

Kolsrud, Oluf, "Korsongen I Nidarosdomen", *Festskrift til O. M. Sandvik. 70-års dagen* (Oslo 1945).

Kolsrud, Oluf, *Noregs kyrkjesoga, I. Millomalderen* (Oslo 1958).

Kortner, Olaf, Munthe, Preben & Tveterås, Egil, (eds.), *Aschehoug og Gyldendals Store Norske Leksikon* (Oslo 1986–89).

Krötzl, Christian, *Pilger, Mirakel und Alltag, Formen des Verhaltens im skandinavischen Mittelalter* (Helsinki 1994).

Kulturhistorisk Leksikon for Nordisk Middelalder (Copenhagen 1956–78).

Lange, Chr. A. & Unger, Carl R., (eds.) *Diplomatarium norvegicum* (Christiania 1855).

Ledang, Ola Kai, (ed.), *Gregorianikk, billedkunst og liturgi i middelalderen* (Trondheim, 1996).

Lillie, Eva Louise, & Petersen, Nils Holger, (eds.), *Liturgy and the Arts in the Middle Ages* (Copenhagen 1996).

Mikkelsen, Egil, "Arabisk sølv og Nordens guder. Islam i vikingfunn", Rindal, Magnus, (ed.) *Fra hedendom til kristendom, perspektiver på religionsskiftet i Norge* (Oslo 1996).

Missale nidrosiense (Copenhagen 1519).

Nedkvitne, Arne, & Norseng, Per G., *Oslo bys historie* (Oslo 1991).

Nicholson, Ranald, *Scotland: The Later Middle Ages. The Edinburgh History of Scotland vol. 1* (Edinburgh 1974).

Nilsson, Bertil, (ed.) *Kristnandet i Sverige. Gamla källor och nya perspektiv* (Uppsala 1996).

Nygård, Mette, *—Og vegjine falle så vide—Om gamle og nye pilgrimsmål* (Oslo 1996).

Ording, Fr. & Boyesen, Einar, *Pedagogikkens Historie* (Oslo 1968).

Ottosen, Knud, *A Short History of the Church of Scandinavia* (Århus 1986).

Ottóson, R.A., (ed.) *Sancti Thorlaci episcopi officia rhytmica et proprium missae in AM241 A folio.* Bibliotheca Arnamagnæana *Supplementum* 3 (Copenhagen 1959).

Powicke, F. M., and Cheney, C. R., *Councils and Synods with other Documents relating to the English Church A.D. 1205–1313* (Oxford 1964).

Rankin, Susan, "From memory to record: musical notations in manuscripts from Exeter," *Anglo-Saxon England,* vol. 13 (1984).

Reiss, Georg, *Musiken ved den middelalderlige Olavsdyrkelse i Norden* (Kristiania 1912).

Rindal, Magnus, (ed.) *Fra hedendom til kristendom, perspektiver på religionsskiftet i Norge* (Oslo 1996).

Robertson, Anne Walters, *The Service-Books of the Royal Abbey of Saint-Denis, Images of Ritual and Music in the Middle Ages* (Oxford 1991).

Sadie, Stanley, (ed.) *The new Grove's dictionary of music and musicians* (London 1980).

Schjøth, Else (trans.) & Dahl, Ellert (Introduction) *Egerias reise til Det Hellige Land* (Oslo 1991).

Solhaug, Arne J., *En undersøkelse av Ny Kgl. Saml, 138 4to. Et islandsk graduale-håndskrift fra det 16. århundre* (1971).

Solli, Brit, "Fra hedendom til kristendom. Religionsskiftet i Norge i arkeologisk belysning", *Viking, Tidsskrift for norrøn arkeologi* vol. 58 (1995).

Storm, Gustav, *Afgifter fra den Norske Kirkeprovins til det Apostoliske Kammer og Kardinalkollegiet 1311–1523 efter Optegnelser i de Pavelige Arkiver* (Christiania 1897).

Sumption, Jonathan, *Pilgrimage, an image of mediaeval religion* (London 1975).

The New English Bible (Oxford 1970).

Williams, Peter, *A New History of the Organ from the Greeks to the Present Day* (London 1980).

Wordsworth, Christopher, *Ceremonies and Processions of the Cathedral Church of Salisbury* (Cambridge 1901).

Øverås, Asbjørn, Erichsen, A. E., & Due, Johan, *Trondheim Katedralskoles Historie 1152–1952* (Trondheim 1952).

From *Galdr* to *Paternoster*—
Norse and Christian Music Practices in Snorri's *Heimskringla*[1]

Ola Kai Ledang

Background

Not much is known about Norwegian music life in the middle ages. While our medieval church music has attracted the interest of a number of musicologists, music in a wider sense—both sacred and secular—during the same period has been the focus of little research.

In his compact yet substantial overview of music and musical instruments in medieval Scandinavia, Bergsagel states that

> literary sources (the *Eddas*, the sagas, and the chronicles) make clear at least that even in Viking times music was recognized as an art, a civilized and civilizing accomplishment that belonged to the ideal education of a cultured man (1993:420).

He follows up with literary references to musical sound and the qualities attributed to it, musical activities, instruments, and musicians, followed by a more comprehensive account of liturgical music. Bergsagel's article convincingly reflects the efforts and research priorities which have shaped our knowledge in this field.

On the one hand, medievalists have searched libraries and archives with a fine-tooth comb in search of hard-to-find liturgical fragments. On the other hand, references to easily accessible Norse (Icelandic and Norwegian) sources on music seem haphazard—and, not surprisingly, the same references are recirculated in most writings. For example, one finds only a few references to Snorri Sturluson's *Heimskringla. The Sagas of the Viking Kings of Norway*—the best known of all Icelandic sagas, and found in most Norwegian homes. In short, ref-

---

[1] The author is indebted to Bjørg and Jeremy Hawthorn for supervising the English text, and to Rósa Thorsteinsdóttir for valuable comments on the Icelandic sources and information on the text font Reykjavik Times.

erences to Norse literature in works on medieval music in Norway seem to be more the outcome of a kind of "random discovery" method with a strong cultural bias, than of systematic source reading.

When I started reading Snorri a few years ago in search of references to music, my expectations were modest. I soon discovered, however, that this source abounds with references to musical activities and musical expressions—references which have not yet found their way into music histories. Snorri fascinates me to such an extent that a preliminary reading of *Heimskringla* has propelled me to start searching through other easily available Norse—that is, mainly Icelandic—sources. The present paper aims at a presentation of some selected music references from Snorri, and some preliminary comments on what we can learn about medieval music life in Norway from this source. It must therefore be read as a glimpse into research in progress.

To study Norse music life is like inquiring into a foreign culture, necessitating an ethnomusicological approach. The perspective must be wide and open, taking into account all sonic utterances beyond verbal language. In my experience, an adequate approach requires one to open a perspective on the cultural soundscape (cf Ledang 1995). Thus, my starting point has been to look for descriptions or comments on not only singing, playing, music activities, instruments, sound tools and music performers, but also the use of sound as a human expression in general, transcending the realm of spoken language and of music in a narrow sense of the word.

It is crucial to avoid projecting one's own attitudes on to the music of past times. The reading has to be explorative; with alertness to unexpected designations, expressions and events which say something about people's relations to sound but which one easily overlooks because they fall outside our own cultural background and sonic experiences. By observing and identifying sound usage outside our own musical realms, one gradually expands one's own perspective while exploring the historical sources. Something happens to the reader during reading: a perspective is unfolded, and one has continuously to revise and expand one's own ideas and understanding of the subject.

Historically speaking, *Heimskringla* covers a period of three centuries, from around 900 to the second part of the 12th century, which includes the far-reaching process of change from old Norse religion to Christianity. Chronology is not, however, a main focus of the present paper, mainly because it requires a much more substantial knowledge of other sources than I have yet acquired. Hopefully, I shall have the opportunity of returning to this interesting and challenging aspect in the future.

Possessing only modest knowledge of the Norse and Icelandic languages, I have mainly based my reading on a modern translation of *Heimskringla* (Snorre 1979). Methodologically, this is a weakness, since expressions with music relevance may have been lost in the translation process. On the other hand, I have consulted the Icelandic text for all references to music and related topics. I have found it convenient to use a standard, published version, edited by the Icelandic scholar Finnur Jónsson (Snorri 1911). Thus, problems related to the interpretation of the original source material have been left out of consideration. Within the present format, it is also not possible to go deeply into a number of important issues, such as Snorri's own knowledge and sources, matters of representativity (did Snorri really describe past Norwegian traditions, or did he extrapolate/project from his contemporary Icelandic society?), or chronology and the historical process.

The abundance of poems—*kvæði*—is only briefly touched upon. These texts are extremely complicated, with an abundance of literary subtleties, examples of poetic licence, and metaphors, large enough to fill an encyclopedia, cf *Lexicon Poeticum*. A thorough study of musical references in these texts, requiring extensive linguistic expertise, must await future investigation.

Skálds, Skaldship and *Kvæði*

In his Foreword, Snorri argues that poems—*kvæði*—are trustworthy testimonies:

> Now when Harald Fairhair was king of Norway, Iceland was settled. At the court of King Harald there were skalds *[skáld]*, and men still remember their poems *[kvæði]* and the poems about all the kings who have since his time ruled in Norway; and we gathered most of our information from what we are told in those poems *[kvæðum]* which were recited before the chieftains themselves or their sons. We regard all that to be true which is found in those poems about their expeditions and battles. It is [to be sure] the habit of poets to give highest praise to those princes in whose presence they are; but no one would have dared to tell them to their faces about deeds which all who listened, as well as the prince himself, knew were only falsehoods and fabrications. That would have been mockery, still not praise (Snorri, Foreword).

Terms such as *skáld*, and *kvæði* are not unambiguous but reflect a conceptual complex which also includes musical elements. *Kvæði* means poem (Norrøn Ordbok 1990:255), whereas *kveða* has different meanings, such as speak, talk, express, speak out (poems) rhythmically and solemnly, sing, compose, sound, scream, resound (ibid.:252). The Norse and Icelandic *skáld* is commonly translated poet but his or her activity, *skáldskapr*, refers not only to making poetry but also to the creation and performance of lampoons (libellous ditties).

Óthin was the most prominent of the Norse gods:

> he spoke so well and so smoothly that all who heard him believed all he said was true. All he spoke was in rimes, as is now the case in what is called skaldship *[skáldskapr]*. He and his temple priests are called songsmiths *[ljóðasmiðir]*, because that art began with them in the northern lands (Saga of the Ynglings, Chapter 6).

The connection between skaldship and songsmiths is important and fundamental. Another facet of the same conceptual complex is the term *ljóð*, with meanings such as verse, stanza, song or magic song, and its derivative, *ljoðatól*, meaning musical instrument. *Skáld*, *skáldskapr*, and *kvæði* thus reflect a conceptual universe where music and sound are granted special importance, not least in religious contexts.

In several places, Snorri tells us that *kvæði* were sung. One instance was when Torodd Snorrason was sent by Óláf Haraldsson to Jemtland to collect taxes. Torodd and his men were captured and guarded by thralls. Torodd sang poems and made fun of the thralls *[kvað kvæði ok skemti þeim þrælunum]*, establishing contact that eventually led to his escape from the unfriendly Swedes! (Saint Óláf's Saga, Chapter 141).

Snorri even gives an example indicating that composing humorous verses was a royal entertainment. During his voyages on the Black Sea and in Russia, King Harald Hardruler found time for such relaxing activities:

> On this journey Harald composed humorous verses *[orti Haraldr gamanvísur]*, sixteen altogether, with one refrain for them all *[ok er eitt niðrlag at ǫllum]* (Saga of Harald Sigurtharson, Chapter 15).

The term *niðrlag*, meaning the end (Norrøn Ordbok 1990:314), in the present context is synonymous with refrain. If the king used the same refrain for all sixteen verses, he was actually composing a ballad. Medieval ballads of similar structure are found in the Norwegian folk tradition up to the 19th century.

Praise Poems

An important function of *kvæði* was to praise the king or some other important figure. Once, when Óláf Haraldsson said he did not understand skaldship, Sigvat Skald spoke a verse ending thus:

> ...
> *and even if thou, king of*
> *all Norway, hast ever*

scorned and scoffed at other
skalds, yet I shall praise thee.
(Saint Òláf's Saga, Chapter 43.)

In the Icelandic text one finds the expression *lofi skalda*—skalds' praise. There is ample evidence that praise words got extra weight when delivered in a rhythmic, verse style—and sometimes even in song.

Snorri also gives evidence of a genre which, at least in its content, was the opposite of the praise poem: the lampoon or libellous ditty. Such verses were in fact considered as a particularly strong form of defamation.

Lampooning Verses: *Nið* and *Niðvísu*

When the Icelanders composed lampooning verses about the Danish king, he got so angry that he formed the intention of taking his army across the sea to punish them:

> Then the king of Denmark had the intention to sail with his fleet to Iceland to avenge the unsult which all Icelanders had heaped on him. It had been put into the laws in Iceland that a lampooning verse about the Danish king be composed for every head in the land. The reason for this was that when a vessel owned by Icelanders was shipwrecked in Denmark, the Danes appropriated all the cargo, calling it goods drifted ashore. And it was a bailiff of the king, called Birgir who was responsible for that. Lampooning verses were composed *[Var nið ort]* about him and the king. Among them *[níðinu]* is this one … (Saga of Óláf Tryggvason, Chapter 33).

The terms *niðvísu* and *yrkja nið* make it clear that this text is really about songs. Such content is confirmed by the landscape law—Frostatingslova (1994:91), going back to the 11th century—in which it is stated that a man who composed/performed only as much as one fourth of a lampooning verse could be taken to court and, if he was found guilty, sentenced to banishment. It also happened that the one who was defamed would revenge himself. King Óláf Tryggvason's Saxon priest Thangbrand, who was sent to preach Christianity in Iceland, met with serious opposition which provoked revenge:

> Thorvald Veili and the skald Vetrlithi composed scurrilous verses *[ortu nið]* about Thangbrand, and he killed both. Thangbrand stayed two years in Iceland and had slain three persons before leaving (Saga of Óláf Tryggvason, Chapter 73).

These skalds did more than compose praise poems, they also wrote scurrilous verses! But did they also compose tunes? Or did they borrow from a common, known repertory of vocal melodies, which could be adapted to new texts?

A practice of this kind is known in Norwegian vocal folk music traditions up to the 20th century.

The penetrating effect attributed to lampoons seems to indicate that people attributed special values and power into songs and singing. This applied to praise as well as to mockery. Skaldic poetry gives strong evidence that poems and songs—words with rhythm and rhyme—were attributed special power. Adding a melody strengthened this power still more. The most striking evidence of this is possibly those instances where singing was associated with magic and sorcery.

Charms and Magic Songs: *Galdr* and *Seið*

Galder or galdresong was a kind of magic song, used within a magico-religious context. Snorri comments on the mythological origin of this tradition. He tells that the Vanir beheaded Mímir and sent the head to the Æsir:

> Óthin took it and embalmed it with herbs so that it would not rot, and spoke charms over it *[kvað þar yfir galdra]*, giving it magic power so that it would answer him and tell him many occult things (Saga of the Ynglings, Chapter 4).

Here, the singing is integrated in a complex interactive pattern. *Galdr* has several meanings, including crowing, singing, and chanting magic charms (Norrøn Ordbok 1990:136); the expression *kvað galdra* most likely indicates magico-religious chanting or singing. It is worth pointing out that in this verbal context, the singing act is not separated out as a distinct phenomenon, either semantically or in terms of activity. The term *galdr,* meaning galdresong, thus reflects a way of thinking and acting where singing does not appear as an autonomous, self-sufficient activity. It was a necessary—and probably very important—element embedded in pre-Christian religious practice.

Óthin also used galdresong for teaching:

> And all these skills *[íþróttir]* he taught with those runes and songs which are called magic songs [charms] *[ljóðum þeim, er galdrar heita]*. For this reason the Æsir are called Workers of Magic (Saga of the Ynglings, Chapter 7).

This pedagogical use of magic songs possibly indicates an awareness of the mnemotechnical potential of singing: imbuing a verbal phrase with rhyme, rhythm, and melody makes it much easier to memorize. Such mnemotechnical practice is well-known in many cultures where oral transmission plays a role.

Needless to say, we know nothing about what galdresong sounded like. A clue to this problem might be the term from which galder is derived: *gala*, meaning crowing. On the other hand, there is strong evidence that the galder was much practised and well-known in Norse society. This practice was shunned by those kings who favoured the new religion:

> King Óláf then proceeded to the town of Túnsberg and held an assembly there at which he proclaimed that all those who were known to be guilty of practicing magic and sorcery or who were warlocks *[því at fœri með galdra ok gørningar, eða seiðmenn]* must leave the country. Then the king had a search made in that neighborhood for such persons, and summoned them to his presence (Saga of Óláf Tryggvason, Chapter 62).

Snorri's Christian outlook is lurking in the background when he puts *galdr*—Norse religious practice—together with *gørningar,* meaning witchcraft (Norrøn Ordbok 1990:143). He follows up with *seiðmenn*, meaning sorcerer, wizard (ibid.:360). *Seiðr* means a kind of witchcraft through singing (idem).

It is no surprise that king Óláf Tryggvason dealt with such persons summarily, by killing those who did not flee the country. We do not know, however, if galdresong went out of use, or if it survived as a subcultural phenomen, outside the realm of the church. The concept of galder has certainly survived in folk culture to modern times. As a religious practice within the public sphere it was obviously replaced by the newcomer: the plain-chant of the church. Before turning to this innovation, we shall continue our inquiry into Norse music culture.

Instrumentalists and Entertainment

Snorri gives several colourful descriptions of social gatherings and parties, involving a profusion of food and drink, and hosts and guests in a lively mood. However, musicians or music are rarely mentioned explicitly.

Players in the King's Court

When musicians are mentioned, they are described in a way indicating low esteem:

> Hugleik was the name of Álf's son who succeeded to the kingdom of Sweden after these brothers; because Yngvi's sons were still children. King Hugleik was no warrior but remained quietly in his kingdom. He was exceedingly wealthy, and miserly of his goods. He was given to have in his retinue all sorts of jugglers, harpers, and fiddlers, and players on the viol *[allz konar leikara, harpara ok gígjara ok fiðlara]*. Also, he had with him sorcerers and all kinds of magicians *[seiðmenn ok allz konar fjǫlkunnigt fólk]* (Saga of the Ynglings, Chapter 22).

The term *leikari* (pl. *leikara*) has various meanings, such as player, juggler, artist, and refers to the wandering all-round artists who were known in many parts of Europe in the middle ages, making their livelihood from entertaining people with instrumental and vocal music and various tricks. The musicians were named after their instruments: harp, gigje and fiddle. What these names really referred to, is a complex organological issue which falls beyond the scope of the present paper.

The description of musicians in King Hugleik's court has a parallel in the story of Earl Ragnvald's visit to the Swedish king in Uppsala. The king invited Ragnvald to a banquet and treated him with great hospitality:

> Then delicacies were brought in, and after that there came in jesters with harps and fiddles and other musical instruments [*ok þar eptir fóru inn leikarar með horpur ok gígjur ok songtól*], and then drinks were served. The king was in almost cheerful mood and had many eminent men as his guests, ... (Saint Óláf's Saga, Chapter 94).

The term *songtól* refers to a type of tool for making sound, most likely it is some sort of musical instrument, but of what kind we cannot know. Here, as in the quotation above, it is noteworthy that *leikarar* is used as the collective term for musicians.

Snorri showed little interest in performing musicians who entertained at social gatherings. But considered in the context of other sources, the two quotations above confirm the use of music for entertainment at parties and banquets.

The Wood Trumpet: *Lúðr*

The use of the wood trumpet—*lúðr*—occurs so frequently and in such a variety of situations in *Heimskringla* that it necessitates a systematic approach to the different contexts, uses, and functions of *lúðr* playing.

To be sure, the lur really refers to a trumpet, because the instrument is always blown. The instrument seems to have been so well-known that Snorri quite often does not even mention the name of the instrument, he only refers to blowing, implying that it was one or more lurs that were blown. Originally, the word *lúðr* referred to a hollowed-out wood log but it was used throughout the Nordic area with the meaning cylindric, blown instrument (Holtsmark 1946).

Since wood was much more readily available in Scandinavia than in Iceland, there is no reason to doubt that Snorri's descriptions of lur playing in the kings' sagas really mirror Norwegian customs. For the sake of comparison: lur playing is hardly mentioned in the Icelandic family sagas I have been able to read so far.

Sounding the Lúðr

The lur was often used as a signal instrument in battles. A classical case is found in the description of the situation right before the battle at Stiklestad started:

> Now when the battle order of the farmers was established, the landed-men spoke to them, exhorting the troops to watch their position, where each one was stationed, beneath which standard was his place, how far from his banner or how near to it. They asked the men to be alert and quick to take their places when the trumpets sounded and they heard the signal *[er lúðrar kvæði við ok herblástr kæmi upp]*, ... (Saint Óláf's Saga, Chapter 223).

As mentioned above, the use of the lur was so common that Snorri often just refers to playing, without specifying the instrument:

> Thereupon Erling had the trumpets blown furiously *[Þá lét Erlingr blása ákafliga]*, bidding his men attack the ships which had not yet been cleared of their crews, saying that they never would have a better chance to avenge King Ingi. Then all raised the battly cry, each urging on the other, and went to the attack (Saga of Magnús Erlingsson, Chapter 7).

In a number of cases, interpreting Snorri's use of the term blowing as an idiomatic expression for blowing the lur presents a problem. This applies particularly to events taking place in Trondheim. According to the oldest Norwegian city law, Bjarkøyretten, documented from the 11th century in Trondheim, the townsmen used horn (that is, horns from animals) for signalling. However, when Snorri refers to blowing on various occasions in Trondheim, the Norwegian translators always take for granted that he means blowing the lur. This is questionable, since the city law is probably the most reliable source when it comes to the situation in Trondheim. Against this background, one might raise the question whether Snorri's use of the term blowing does not always refer to blowing the lur. This interpretational issue seems to have been overlooked by the Norwegian translators of *Heimskringla*. As for the English translation quoted in the present paper, the use of various terms such as trumpet and horn when Snorri only mentions blowing, appears rather inconsistent—but this issue is not discussed here.

In some cases, Snorri makes it clear that it was the king (or some other chief or nobleman) who ordered someone to blow the lur. But who played—was it a person with special qualifications who had this task, or could it be carried out by anybody? In general, Snorri puts the emphasis on the use of the lur, and on the fact that its sound had an important communicative function. In a few instances, however, he refers to the player as a person—*luðrsveininn*—the lur swain. This person was given the task of blowing the lur, but Snorri says nothing about his qualifications, whether he had special training or a special gift for lur blowing.

The lur was often used in battles. Its sound could also reach the enemy and thus warn them that something was going on. King Hákon was once warned in this way, the enemy coming from behind:

> But Hákon had barely arrived at Véey Island when they heard blasts of trumpets *[er þeir heyrðu lúðragang]*, because the ships nearest to Eindrithi's turned around, wanting to help him, and both sides gave battle just as opportunity offered (Saga of Magnús Erlingsson, Chapter 7).

The plural *lúðragang* tells that the sound came from several lurs.

Summoning People by Sounding the Lur

Often, lur playing was used to bring people together. Sometimes, the sounding was directed only at a particular, limited group. This happened, for example, once in Trondheim, when the priest Thangbrand's report about his unsuccessful mission to Iceland infuriated King Óláf Tryggvason:

> The king became so furiously angry that he had the trumpets sounded to summon all Icelanders then in the town *[hann lét blása ǫllum íslenzkum mǫnnum saman]*, and said that all were to be killed (Saga of Óláf Tryggvason, Chapter 84).

The sounding of the instruments (whether they were lur or horn, is an open question) in this instance conveyed two messages: 1) it was directed at Icelanders only, and 2) they were to be summoned. Or perhaps blowing the instruments was combined with a verbal message that only the Icelanders should assemble? Snorri does not give the answer. Another time, the king had his own people summoned in this way:

> There was a certain man by the name of Thóraldi who was the king's steward on his estate at Haug. ... The king summoned him to talk with him in private ... "I am told about the ways of the people in the inner reaches of the Trondheimsfjord, and is it true that they perform sacrifices? I want you to tell me what are the facts," the king said, "as you know them. You owe me that, for you are my man." Thóraldi replied, ... "To tell the truth, sire, if you want the facts, in the interior of the Trondheim District nearly all the people are pure heathen in their belief, even though some few are baptized. It is their custom to perform a sacrifice in the fall to welcome winter, a second at midwinter, an a third in summer to welcome its arrival. ..." Now when the king had learned the truth, he had the trumpets blown to summon his troops *[þó lét hann blása saman liði sínu]*, and ordered them to board the ships (Saint Óláf's Saga, Chapter 109).

It is perhaps significant that in this case, summoning the troops together by sounding a wind instrument happened spontaneously, in a situation where fast action was considered necessary. One also should notice that the sound tool was only used to summon people together, whereas the order to board the ships was apparently given in spoken language. This pattern seems to reflect a common practice, in which case one did not need a repertory of various wind-instrument signals for the various occasions and practical needs.

Before and during a battle, signals were blown in various situations:

> Then the king had the trumpets blown for all his army to gather *[Lét konungr þá blása saman ǫllum herinum]*, and all men put on their armor and lay under the open sky at night beneath their shields; because they were told that the army of the Wends had come near. ... / ...
> Then King Magnús arose and ordered the trumpets to be blown for the army to arise *[kallaði, at blása skyldi herblástr]*. By that time the host of the Wends was advancing towards them over the river (Saga of Magnús the Good, Chapter 26/28).

In general, blowing the lur was a means of getting people together in special situations, such as when there was a threat, or something dramatic had just happened, or one had to fight. Sounding wind instruments for an assembly was also common.

Sounding for an Assembly

Lurs and lur blowers must have followed the king everywhere. During his talks with the Orkney earls, Óláf Haraldsson summoned a meeting:

> When King Óláf had reflected on this whole matter, he had the trumpets blown for an assembly to be attended by as many as possible *[lét hann blása til fjǫlmennrar stefnu]*, and had the two earls called to be present (Saint Óláf's saga, Chapter 102).

Apparently, the blowing only signalled an upcoming event: the earls were called in person. A similar situation is described in Bergen, when Erling was there with many ships and wanted to get a chance to speak to the skippers of the merchant ships:

> But on a certain day Erling summoned the skippers to a meeting *[En einn hvern dag lét Erlings blása til stýrimanna stefnu]* ... (Saga of Magnús Erlingsson, Chapter 5).

The same procedure was also practised in Trondheim:

> Early next morning Erling gave the signal for all the troops to assemble at Eyrar *[lét Erlingr blása ǫllu liðinu út á Eyrar til þings]*, and at this assembly Erling accused the people of Trondheim of treason against the king and himself, ... (Saga of Magnús Erlingsson, Chapter 26).

In the last case, however, it is hard to say if the *blása* of the original text refers to lur or to horn, since Bjarkøyretten prescribed horn as the signalling instrument in Trondheim. Perhaps the horn was the instrument of the townsmen, whereas the lur was used by the king? This puzzling problem is manifest in a number of descriptions from Trondheim, in which Snorri does not specify what kind of instrument one used. This applies, for example, to the following incident:

> Then the king got up and had the trumpet blown for a gathering of his retinue *[ok lét blása til hirðstefnu]*, ... (Saint Óláf's Saga, Chapter 83).

However, judging from a number of references where the instrument is specified, the lur seems to have been obligatory in battles.

Sounding the Battle Call

Once, when King Hákon was in port with 14 ships, a warning of Erling's approach with 21 ships prompted Hákon to order his troops to the ships in a hurry:

> Then they hurried to the men who were disporting themselves; and forthwith the trumpet was blown and the battle call sounded for all the troops to go on board the fastest they could *[því næst kvað lúðr við ok var blásinn herblástr ǫllu liði til skipa]* (Saga of Magnús Erlingsson, Chapter 6).

Despite his numerous references to lur sound and lur blowing, Snorri never comments on how this instrument was constructed or what it looked like. Archeological evidence is also scanty but we have at least one interesting find. In the Oseberg ship, dated c. 830 A.D., a straight wooden cylinder was found, which can hardly be anything other than a lur. It is hollowed out and made from two halves. Traces of ribbon-like binding indicate that the tube has been bound together, possibly with linen, hemp or leather strings (only the wood core remains). At one end, the hole is widened, at the other it is narrow, with traces of a ridge indicating a mouthpiece-like design. As a whole, the object reminds one of the birch-bark lurs we know from mountain farming, except for its more rugged design and different binding.

The Oseberg find indicates that the lur was well established as a viking sound tool long before most of the events described in *Heimskringla* took place. Seen together, this find and Snorri's numerous references to the use of the lur as a signalling instrument, strongly suggest that the lur was a commonly used instrument during the viking period and well into the 12th century. The significance of the lur persisted even longer than that which can be inferred from Snorri; in the saga of the famous King Sverre (not in *Heimskringla*), the king's lur is even referred to as having a name, Andvake. And it becomes clear that the sound—or was it the sight, or both?—of Andvake induced fear in Sverre's enemies and enthusiasm in his own troops. This confirms the importance of the lur well into the late 12th century.

Judged from Snorri, sounding the battle call was a must. For example, when Magnús Bareleg was fighting the Irish:

> Then Eyvind spoke. "Sir king," he said, "our troops are faring badly. Let us quickly hit on a good plan." The king said, "Let a blast of trumpets call all the troops under their banners *["blási herblástr ǫllu liðinu undir merkin"]*; but let all those who are here form a rampart of shields, ... (Saga of Magnús Barelegs, Chapter 25).

The widespread use of wind instruments for signalling purposes—and, as pointed out, in many cases Snorri does not explicitly mention the lur, only the translators do—might call forth a suspicion that animal horns were also commonly used. Snorri mentions blowing the horn only exceptionally. On one occasion, when Saint Óláf's delegate Karle went to Bjarmeland and made a surprise attack to destroy a statue of the deity Jomale, it is reported that the guards blew their horns immediately *[ok blésu þegar í horn sín]*, and then they heard lurs sounding from all directions *[því næst heyrðu þeir lúðragang alla vega frá sér]* (Saint Óláf's Saga, Chapter 133). In this case, there seems to have been a differentiated use of lur and horn. Perhaps the guards used the horn to be more mobile, whereas the lur was blown by stationary personnel.

Sounding to Go Ashore, and for the Men to Repair to the Ships

On their warlike expeditions with many ships, the kings sounded wind instruments as a convenient means of keeping their troops in good order. Harald Hardruler made use of his musicians when he took his troops ashore in England:

> On Monday, when Harald Sigurtharson had eaten his fill at breakfast, he ordered the trumpets to be blown for going ashore *[þá lét hann blása til landgǫngu]*. He got his army ready, deciding which troops were to go with him and which were to stay behind (Saga of Harald Sigurtharson, Chapter 87).

The troops were also summoned down to the ships in this way. Sometimes they were in a hurry, as when Erling Skjalgsson and Óláf Haraldsson were chasing each other:

> And as soon as Erling became aware that the king came sailing from the east he gave the horn signal for all his men to come down to the ships *[þá lét hann blása liði sínu ǫllu til skipanna]*. Then all his men boarded the ships and prepared for battle (Saint Óláf's Saga, Chapter 175).

Exceptionally, it also happened that the crew grumbled against being summoned by means of the lur:

> On Tuesday during Rogation Week Erling had trumpet signals given that the crews were to repair to the ships *[Týsdag í gagndǫgum lét Erlingr blása liði sínu til skipa]*, but the men were unwilling to leave the town and thought it was hard to pull against the wind (Saga of Magnús Erlingsson, Chapter 25).

Summoning the Ships Together

One is tempted to ask if the wood lur was preferred to the animal horn in ships and on the sea, simply because it would float if lost in the water. In any case, there are several reports which confirm that the lur was commonly used onboard ships—this instrument must also have been used for orders about how to manoeuver the ships. Snorri tells that before the battle at Svolder, King Óláv had all his ships summoned together in this way *["Óláfr konungr lét blása til samlǫgu ǫllum skipum sínum"]* (Saga of Óláf Tryggvason, Chapter 103).

Signalling was no doubt the foremost function of blowing the lur. However, when Snorri sometimes uses the expression "the king's lur", perhaps it indicates that this special instrument also had a representative function?

The King's *Lúðr*

It is a puzzling fact that Snorri occasionally refers to the king's lur, as if this instrument had some special function or meaning:

> It was on Sunday that Erling had given the merchantmen permission to leave from Bergen, and on Tuesday, as soon as the matins had been sung, a signal was given by the trumpet on the royal ship *[var blásit konungs lúðri]* summoning both troops and townsmen to launch the ships that previously had been pulled ashore. Erling called a meeting with his troops … (Saga of Magnús Erlingsson, Chapter 5).

In the original text, the expression *konungs lúðri* calls forth a suspicion that this really was a special lur. Perhaps it was decorated in some special way? Or was it longer, thus sounding deeper and different from other lurs? The questions queue up but Snorri's answer seems to be that there was nothing unusual about the king's lur. Right after his reference to the king's lur (quoted above), Snorri continues as if it were an ordinary lur:

> Then they hurried to the men who were disporting themselves; and forthwith the trumpet was blown and the battle call sounded for all the troops to go on board *[því næst kvað lúðr við ok var blásinn herblástr ǫllu liði til skip*a] the fastest they could (Saga of Magnús Erlingsson, Chapter 6).

The Lúðr as an Instrument of Torture

Óláf Tryggvason used his lur in a rather cunning way when he tortured the heathen Rauth the Red to death:

> Rauth cried out against him and said he would never believe in Christ, and he uttered much blasphemy. Then the king became enraged and promised him a most terrible death.

Then the king had him tied with his back to a beam with a stick as gag between his teeth to keep his mouth open. Then he had a snake put before his mouth but it wriggled away, because Rauth blew against it. Then the king had the hollow stem of an angelica-stalk put into his mouth—though some say the king had his trumpet put into his mouth *[konungr léti taka lúðr sinn ok setja í munn honum]*—and inserted the snake into it, then applied a glowing iron bar without. Then the snake wriggled into Rauth's mouth and throat and gnawed its way out through his side. From that Rauth died (Saga of Óláf Tryggvason, Chapter 80).

Even if one reads this fantastic story as a myth—and there is much that points in this direction—the treatment of the king's lur is worth a comment. A lur that could be used (or alleged to be used) in this rough way as an instrument of torture, would it not have to be sturdy and built to endure rough treatment rather than lavishly decorated, and fit to be treated as a decorative art object?

Why So Much on Blowing the *Lúðr?*

The abundance of references to blowing the lur (and, possibly, in some cases, the horn) probably reflects the practical importance of this sound tool in battle and to summon people. It is noteworthy that Snorri often uses an expression with emphasis on the active use, stating that the king or the leader "ordered the trumpets to be blown", "gave the horn signal", "had trumpet signals given" etc. The significance of sounds from outdoor instruments such as the lur and the horn in medieval Norway is best thought of with reference to the soundscape, which was generally low-voiced and dominated by sounds of nature. The sound of the lur and the horn was strong and loaded with information and meaning, something everybody noticed and adapted himself to. Snorri's descriptions of blowing the lur (or the horn) thus reveal basic information about sound communication.

Needless to say, Snorri always referred to the lur as a tool for communicating orders and messages—never as a musical instrument and never as an aesthetic object. Its use was utilitarian: lur sound carried action-loaded information. On the other hand, the sound of the lur may just as well have had aesthetic qualities—just as, for example the viking ships were beautiful pieces of art in addition to being vessels for the transport of people and goods.

A concept of music as some kind of self-sufficient, autonomous phenomenon does not appear in *Heimskringla*; in general, musical element are integrated with other, more complex concepts, such as *galder*, *kvede*, and *niðvísu*. And whereas instruments such as the harp, gigje and fiddle occur in social contexts where one used instrumental music for entertainment and possibly, dance, the lur is exclusively described as a signal instrument. Both lur and horn were typical outdoor-instruments, with a loud and probably piercing sound which could be heard at long distances. Both instrument types have survived in mountain farming, whereas use of the birch-bark lur and the horn is documented well into the 20th century. The magnificent bronze horns, found in the Nordic countries, provide evidence that such trumpets have traditions dating back to the Bronze Age. Snorri's references to the lur and the horn fit nicely into a long-lasting instrumental tradition in Scandinavia.

In battle, the lur had several functions: to signal orders, to encourage one's own troops and to frighten the enemy. The battle cry and beating on the shields were other elements in this martial soundscape.

The Battle Cry and the Beating of Shields

Like the sound of the lur, the battle cry must have been a content-loaded sound event standing out in the soundscape.

Snorri describes the dramatic context of battle cry in few words:

> Thereupon Erling had the trumpets blown furiously, bidding his men attack the ships which had not yet been cleared of their crews, saying that they never would have a better chance to avenge King Ingi. Then all raised the battle cry *[þá œpðu allir heróp]*, each urging on the other, and went to the attack (Saga of Magnús Erlingsson, Chapter 7).

The function of the battle cry is here clearly stated to be the encouragement of one's own troops. Snorri says nothing about the response from the enemy. Presumably, an inferior or unprepared enemy would react with fear, whereas a well prepared enemy would be urged to fight by the battle cry from the attacker. The use of loud sounds as a psychological weapon to frighten an enemy is, of course, well known—one immediately thinks of instruments such as bagpipes and drums. The battle cry, as described by Snorri, thus mirrors widespread cultural practices.

Snorri also reveals situations where pre-Christian and Christian practices—and values—combine into a cluster of magical rites:

> Erling bade his men sing the Lord's Prayer *[syngva Pater noster]* and pray that they might be victors who had the right on their side. Then all sang the Kyrie Eleison aloud *[Þá sungu þeir kirjál allir hátt]* and beat on their shields with their swords *[ok bǫrðu vápnum allir á skjǫldu sína]*.
>
> Hearing this din, some three hundred of Sigurth's men took to flight. Erling and his men forded the creek, and Earl Sigurth's men raised their battle cry *[en jarls menn œpðu*

heróp], but nothing came of their rushing down the hill at Erling's ranks, and the battle started in front of the ridge (Saga of Magnús Erlingsson, Chapter 14).

Erling apparently made use of every known spiritual and physical means to win! He started with the most magical of Christian expressions, the Latin Paternoster and the Greek Kyrie, followed by the ear-splitting noise of weapons beating on the shields, and against this, the earl's men raised the battle cry—all before the battle itself began. In his succinct way, Snorri here describes a dramatic encounter between fundamental Christian values and Norse mentality, substantiated in the collective behaviour of Erling's troops and the response from Earl Sigurth's men. The situation is also a thought-provoking example of contemplative singing and of the effective use of the expressive qualities of sound, all in a martial context.

Singing During Work

Snorri was little concerned with daily life and did not say much about musical expressions within the family sphere. He did report an interesting observation, however: an incident where beautiful singing in fact triggered a connection with long-lasting consequences. The main male character, King Sigurth, was known for his acquaintances with women:

> King Sigurth with his following rode east in Vík on his king's progress, and past the estate of a wealthy man by the name of Símon. And as the king rode through the yard he heard someone sing so beautifully *[þá heyrði í hús nǫkkut kveðandi svá fagra]* that he was much pleased. He rode to that house and looked in and saw a woman standing by a handmill and singing wondrously fine while she ground *[þar stóð kona ein við kvern ok kvað við forkunnar fagrt, er hon mól]*. The king descended from his horse and went in and lay with the woman. But when he departed, farmer Símon got to know what the king had been about there. The woman's name was Thóra, and she was a working woman of farmer Símon. Afterwards he had her work done by others. Later on she bore a son, and this boy was named Hákon and termed the son of King Sigurth (Saga of Ingi, Chapter 18).

Snorri's description of singing during work as something normal points to the use of singing as a general human expression within the family sphere as a well-established cultural practice. Such practice was apparently part of the king's own background—and he seems to have had a specially good ear for women's singing.

The original Icelandic text does not use the term singing but the expressions *nǫkkut kveðandi svá fagra* and *kvað við forkunnar fagrt;* such phraseology precisely relates the singing to a Norse context. The term singing—*syngva*—

was used by Snorri only in connection with the vocal music that came with the church, the *cantus gregorianus*.

Holy Mass and Hymn Singing

There is ample evidence in *Heimskringla* that liturgical singing was a duty for the cleric, with the king and his men, and the common people as more or less passive listeners or bystanders. Right from the very beginning, the king "had mass sung":

> Then Óláf sailed east across the sea and sighted land at the Island of Mostr, which was the first place for him to come ashore and where he had mass sung in a tent *[ok lét hann messu þar syngva i landtjaldi]*. In after times a church was built in that same place (Saga of Óláf Tryggvason, Chapter 47).

Snorri's term *messu* shows that the conversion to Christianity also brought new words and concepts to the Norse language. But he also used other terms for the holy service:

> On the morning after, when the king was dressed, he had mass sung for himself *[lét hann syngva sér tíðir]*; and when it was finished *[ok er messu var lokit]* he had the horns blown to summon men for a meeting (Saga of Óláf Tryggvason, Chapter 67).

The term *tíðir* in the original text apparently refers to the officium. It appears that Snorri was not much concerned about the distinction between officium and mass.

Not surprisingly, mass, officium, and liturgy are nowhere mentioned as frequently as in Saint Óláf's Saga. King Óláf Haraldsson is pictured as an unusually pious man, attending mass and officium as often as possible.

> It was the habit of the king to rise betimes in the morning, to put on his clothes and wash his hands, then to go to church and listen to the matins and morning mass *[ganga síðan til kirkju ok hlýða óttusǫng ok morgontíðum]*, then to go to meetings and reconcile people ... (Saint Óláf's Saga, Chapter 58).

However, Snorri also tells of others who attended the holy service, giving evidence that the new religion affected the life of most people. Grégóriús Dagsson was able to include both matins and the reading of the gospel when he stayed overnight in Fors in Sweden:

> Grégóriús ... left Konungahella toward the end of Yule with a large force. They arrived at Fors on the thirteenth day of Yule, and lodged there overnight. He had the matins read for him on the last day of Yule *[hafði þar óttusǫng affardag]*, and afterwards, the gospel *[var honum lesit guðspjall eptir]* (Saga of Hákon the Broadshouldered, Chapter 14).

Christian ceremonies are rarely touched upon. Again, an exception is made for Saint Óláf. On one occasion, when he went to mass *[Óláfr konungr gekk til há-*

messu] on Holy Thursday, there was a procession led by the the bishop, who led the king to his seat on the northern side of the chancel *[leiddi byskup konung til sætis síns fyrir norðan í kórnum]* (Saint Óláf's Saga, Chapter 84).

According to Snorri, the Christian impact was also felt in musical usage outside the church. This applies, for example, to the various activities around the celebrations of Saint Óláf, appealing to pilgrims as well as to the common people. Snorri also tells of prominent figures singing psalms. Among the best known was Sigurth Gadabout-Deacon, who sang many psalms when he was slain in the most horrible way:

> Hall relates that … it took a man of rare strength of mind to stand being tortured in such fashion as not to say a word or to budge; nor did he raise his voice anymore than if he sat drinking. He did not speak with a higher or lower voice, nor more tremulously, than was his custom. He spoke until the very last, and sang a third part of the psalter *[þriðjung ór psalteríó]*. Hall thought that betokened endurance and strength beyond that of other men (Saga of Ingi, Chapter 12).

In various ways, *Heimskringla* throws some light on how liturgical chant affected the lives of people. If we assume that Snorri did not project contemporary cultural practices into his descriptions of earlier times, attending church services seems to have been established as a common practice very quickly. Soon, parts of the liturgy were memorized by chiefs as well as by commoners and established as common knowledge anybody could have recourse to whenever the need was felt. One must remember that the culture was basically oral, favouring attentiveness towards sonic expressions and ability to memorize, use and integrate such expressions in day-to-day life. It is perhaps not surprising that scholars claim to have found traces of Gregorian motifs in Norwegian vocal folk music.

Snorri's use of the verb sing—*syngva*—exclusively in connection with the mass also indicates that liturgical singing had a significant conceptual influence, providing the act of singing with a new status as an activity more self-sufficient and autonomous than it had previously held.

Ringing the Bells and Sounds of Church Bells

Bells, ringing the bells and the sounds of bells came with the Christian church and have influenced the cultural soundscape just as much as the mass, offices and ceremonies. When Óláf Haraldsson was once woken up by bells ringing in the middle of the night, his first thought was that it was time for matins:

> Then Sigvat went to the church, roused the verger, and bade him ring the bell for the souls of the king's men *[bað hann hringja fyrir sál hirðmanna konungs]* who had been killed and mentioned their names. The verger *[Klokkarinn]* did as he was told. But at this tolling *[hringingina]* the king awoke and sat up. He asked if it was time for matins (Saint Óláf's Saga, Chapter 83).

The holiday was regularly announced by church bells. In general, the sounds of church bells called forth good feelings and could be an auspicious sign for the future. The night before the battle at Lyrskogs Heath, King Magnús the Good had a dream in which his father, Saint Óláf, promised to help him in the battle and said that he and his troops should

> "Go to battle when you hear my horn" *[er þér heyrið lúðr minn]*. But when the king awoke he told [the men about him] his dream. Then it was bright daylight. Then all the army heard the ringing of a bell aloft, and those of King Magnús' men who had been in Nitharós thought that it sounded like the pealing of Gloth *[Glad]*. That was the bell King Óláf had given the Church of Saint Clement in Kaupang (Saga of Magnús the Good, Chapter 27).

In a unique way, this incident illustrates similarities and differences in old and new concepts of sound and sound tools. A strong sense of symbolism is embedded in the manifestation of Saint Óláf's lur as the sound from a well-known church bell in Kaupang (Trondheim). The warlike lur call for battle was replaced by the sounds of a bell, the messenger of the church and of Saint Óláf!

A relevant background for this incident is provided by the following description of the symbolic content of the sounds of bells:

> Thórarin Loftunga was in attendance with King Svein at the time, and saw and heard these great miracles, witnessing to the sanctitude of King Óláf: that above his sanctuary one could hear sounds as church bells were rung by supernatural powers *[dómi hljóm, svá sem klukkur hringðisk]*; and candles lit themselves above the altar, kindled by heavenly fire (Saint Óláf's Saga, Chapter 245).

Every church was supposed to have at least one bell; this is confirmed by the Frostatingslova (1994:20, II.8). Snorri mentions that King Harald Sigurtharson sent a church bell to Island *[sendi út hingat klukku]*, for the church built from timber sent by Saint Óláf (Saga of Harald Sigurtharson, Chapter 36). He also wrote about the *Bæjarbót* (meaning city helper) bell in Nidaros (Trondheim):

> King Óláf established the Great Guild in Nitharós, and many others in the market towns. Before, there had been only banquets at various places. Bœjarbót was the name of the great guild bell in Nitharós *[þá var Bæjarbót in mikla hvirfingsklokka i Niðarósi]*. The guild brothers there built the Church of Saint Margaret, a stone church (Saga of Óláf Kyrre, Chapter 2).

In sum, *Heimskringla* gives evidence that church bells and their sounds made a strong impact on the Norwegian soundscape. Church bells drowned out all other sonic elements in the cultural soundscape of the middle ages, to such an extent that this "sacred noise" (an expression coined by the Canadian composer and musicologist Murray Schafer) was even noticed by the saga writer Snorri.

Conclusion

The descriptions and comments in this paper are tentative and must be read as little more than samples from work in progress. The most important experience drawn from these preliminary samples is perhaps that the people in Snorri's *Heimskringla* made active and conscious use of music and other sonic expressions. They demonstrated a keen sense of aesthetic and emotional values in liturgical singing and in beautiful singing within the family sphere. They used instrumentalists at parties, presumably for entertainment and perhaps for dancing (the term dance is not used by Snorri, but appears in later sources). They exploited the expressive power of sound in the battle cry and in beating on their shields and they utilized the communicative potential of sound in blowing the lur in a variety of situations and contexts.

I have tried to approach this whole cultural complex profitably from an ethnomusicological angle, aiming at a holistic view of music in a wide perspective. From a general point of view, the soundscape concept provides a useful tool for revealing how people took advantage of the aesthetical, expressive and emotional qualities and communicative potential of sound, and how music manifested itself in a broad spectrum of sound events.

In a striking way, *Heimskringla* is focused on descriptions of music as an expression of power. Snorri's references to charms and magic songs, praise poems and lampooning verses generally appear as elements in stories about power and physical conflict. Even references to liturgical singing, psalms and church bells often derive from power structures, and the battle call and battle cry are firmly based in the exercise of force.

Snorri's focus on utilitarian uses of music in most—if not all—cases reflects his general priorities; a multitude of other uses actually fall beyond his thematic horizon and are therefore non-themes in *Heimskringla*.

As touched upon above, my conclusions are preliminary and open to future revision based on extended source studies. Significant information on Medieval music and music life, not yet put into operation in musicological studies, are probably still concealed in easily accessible Norwegian and Icelandic writings.

References

Bergsagel, John: "Music and Musical Instruments", *Medieval Scandinavia An Encyclopedia*, p. 420–423. New York and London 1993.

Bjarkøyretten: *Bjarkøyretten. Nidaros eldste bylov*, translated by Jan Ragnar Hagland and Jørn Sandnes. Oslo 1997.

Frostatingslova: *Frostatingslova*, translated by Jan Ragnar Hagland and Jørn Sandnes. Oslo 1994.

Holtsmark, Anne: "Det norrøne ord lúðr", *Maal og minne* 1946:49–65.

Norrøn Ordbok: *Norrøn ordbok*, 4th edition of Gamalnorsk ordbok, edited by Leiv Heggstad, Finn Hødnebø and Erik Simensen, Oslo 1990.

Lexicon Poeticum: *Lexicon Poeticum antiquæ linguæ septentrionalis*. Ordbog over det norsk-islandske skjaldesprog oprindelig forfattet af Sveinbjörn Egilsson. Forøget og påny udgivet for Det kongelige nordiske oldskriftselskab ved Finnur Jonsson. 2. utg. Copenhagen 1931.

Ledang, Ola Kai: "The Soundscape—Progenitor of Music and Instruments", in *Studia Instrumentorum Musicae Popularis*, Vol XI (1995).

Snorre Sturluson: *Norske kongesoger*, translated by Steinar Schjøtt and Hallvard Magerøy and edited by Finn Hødnebø and Hallvard Magerøy, Oslo 1979.

Snorri Sturluson: *Heimskringla Nóregs Konunga Sǫgur*, edited by Finnur Jónsson, Copenhagen 1911.

Snorri: *Heimskringla.The Sagas of the Viking Kings of Norway*, translated by Lee M. Hollander. Oslo 1987.

Cantus Sororum—Seven Offices in Honour of the Virgin Mary Within the Bridgettine Order

Viveca Servatius

Ordo sancti Salvatoris, the Order of the Most Holy Saviour, founded by the Holy Bridget—Birgitta—(ca 1303–1373), was—according to the rule—to consist of 60 nuns and 25 *fratres,* of which 17 were priests and deacons whose commission it was to serve the nuns with mass, confession and sermons. Contrary to an often expressed opinion it was not a double order, but a nuns convent with the abbess at its head and the confessor general in a subordinate position to her. From the mother abbey in Vadstena the order spread during the Middle Ages throughout Scandinavia and Europe.

St. Bridget laid down strict rules for the services of the common monastery church, in which the nuns had their choir in a high gallery facing east and the brethren had their places behind the high altar in the western choir.

The sisters were to sing a specially conceived office in honour of the Virgin Mary, the *Cantus sororum* (Chant of the Sisters) also called The Virgin Mary's Garden. The brethren were to sing the office of the diocese.[1] Their hours succeeded one another throughout the day, first the brethren, then the sisters. The two convents were linked together once a day in the hymn *Ave maris stella* which was sung alternately between the vespers of the brethren and that of the sisters.[2]

The Cantus sororum consists of seven small offices or *historiæ*; one *historia* for each day of the week. The model is *Officium parvum Beatae Marie Virginis* (BMV), the small Marian additional office, which according to common practice is said/sung before and as an introduction to the main office. But instead of having the sisters sing the Marian offices as an introduction to the main offices of the brethren, the Cantus sororum formed the main office. Accordingly the chant of the sisters was to be sung more slowly than that of the brethren as a sign of greater solemnity. The diocesan office was thus 'reduced'

---

1 In Vadstena the office of the diocese of Linköping.
2 Huebner 1973, p 87 f.

to the role of introductory office. This reversed order makes the Cantus sororum a special case from a liturgical history point of view.

The basis of the Cantus sororum consists of those revelations of St. Bridget that are called *Sermo angelicus*. They also form the readings at matins. This 'Dictation of the Angel', which St. Bridget received and wrote during the many years she was staying in Rome, tells in seven parts of the Holy Mother of God, her life and deeds in relation to her Son. They also are the thematic starting points for the texts of the chants.

The first three *historiæ* describe the joy of the Triune God, the angels, the patriarchs and the prophets over the future birth of the Virgin Mary. For Wednesday the readings are about Mary's parents, her birth and her childhood. Those for Thursday are about the annunciation and the birth of Christ. For Friday the readings describe Mary's suffering in connection with the crucifixion. Finally, the *historia* of Saturday is about the death of Mary and her ascension.

The person who at St. Bridget's bidding undertook the task of compiling texts and melodies, prayers and other cantillations was her father confessor, master *Petrus Olavi* of Skänninge (+1378). He was also the first confessor general of the Vadstena abbey. Close collaboration between Bridget and master Petrus can be seen in the realisation of the Cantus sororum. This work was carried out in Rome some time between 1353–1366.[3] Master Petrus also compiled the chants for the daily mass in honour of the Holy Virgin. These were borrowed from outside, whereas the chants of the offices, according to need, were taken from the common Gregorian repertory, or made up by Petrus himself.

The authorship can be regarded as certain. Both St. Bridget's own statements and the diary of the Vadstena monastery[4] name master Petrus as the man who has compiled/composed[5] the Cantus sororum. St. Bridget writes: "It was granted him to compose that chant, which is that gold, which is to give solace unto many",[6] and further, writing the words of the Mother of God:

> Say unto him, who writes my praise, not for his own glory or reward, but in honour of him who is worthy of all praise for all his deeds that as the princes of this world give worldly recompense to their eulogists, I will give him spiritual reward. For as one single syllable has many notes over it, so it deigns God to give him in heaven crowns for each and every syllable that is in the chant and it shall be said about him: "Behold, the singer of praises comes, he who composed a chant with no thought of worldly reward, but only for the glory of God."[7]

---

3   Collins 1969, p xxviii ff.
4   V. Gejrot 1988, p. 119.
5   In the sources the verb *componere* is used. V. Servatius 1990:1, p 215–234.
6   *Revelationes extravagantes* chapter 6; ed. Hollman 1956, p. 119.
7   *Revelationes extravagantes* chapter 7; ed. Hollman 1956, p. 120.

The melodies for the Cantus sororum are to be found in two groups of sources from the 15th and the beginning of the 16th centuries. The first group consists of Swedish manuscripts; 12 *directoria chori* from the Vadstena monastery[8] which, with the odd exception, only contain *initia*, i.e. the first, initial notes of the chants. All Swedish *antiphonaria* have been lost in connection with the reformation. Only six fragments of *antiphonaria* with a few chants have been preserved in the form of parchment book covers.[9]

The problematic situation as regards the Swedish source material necessitates the investigation of manuscripts from foreign Bridgettine monasteries. Thus one *antiphonarium* comes from Italy,[10] six from Bavaria,[11] three from the Netherlands[12] and one from the north German area.[13] To this material can be added some processionals of German provenance, which contain a few chants from the Cantus sororum.[14]

All sources are written in square notation, except the north German one which is written in German notation. The Bavarian mss are in square notation, this in an area where the gothic types of notation was the norm, excepting certain religious orders.[15]

The *historia* of any given day of the week contains the *invitatorium*, three great responsories, 13 antiphons to psalms and the New Testament canticles, eight hymns and one troped *Benedicamus Domino*. Within this material the melodies for the antiphons, hymns and the *Benedicamus* tropes have been examined and ordered.[16] As regards the hymns all melodies are borrowed from outside, while most of the texts are written specifically for the Cantus sororum.[17]

The all in all 91 antiphons are of special interest as they represent a cross section of the methods master Petrus used to compile the Cantus sororum. According to need they were collected from feasts of the Blessed Virgin such as *Conceptio BMV* or *Assumptio BMV*. The *historia* of Thursday (birth of Christ) was also easily provided for from the common repertory. For this reason most of

8   University library of Uppsala C 433, C 442, C 458, C 468, C 470, C 472, C 473, C 482, C 483, C 485, C 508, Linköpings Lands- och Stiftsbibl. T 229.
9   Kept in Riksarkivet, Stockholm; v. Servatius 1990:2, p. 60–63.
10   Since 1983 in Stockholm Kungl. Biblioteket with the signum A 84.
11   Altomünster, Klosterbibliothek, MS P An 1–6; with the exception of the last ms, these mss come from the neighbouring Bridgetine monastery Maria Maihingen.
12   Uden, Birgitinessen Abdij Marie Refugie Ms K An 1, Ms K An 2; Uden, Museum voor Religieuze Kunst, Ms 072.
13   Paris, Bibliothèque Nationale, Mus. Rés. F 696–697.
14   Stockholm, Kungl. Biblioteket A 92a; München, Universitätsbibliothek 4° Ms 176.
15   Servatius 1990:2, p. 47 f.
16   Servatius 1990:2; Nilsson 1991, p. 91–120; Servatius 1977 (unpublished).
17   V. Nilsson 1991, p. 99.

the antiphons for the *historiae* of Wednesday, Thursday and Saturday are borrowed material.

More difficult was the conception of the offices of Sunday, Monday and Tuesday, where God and the hosts of heaven rejoice in the future birth of the Virgin Mary. As such feasts did not exist, the only option was to create new texts and music. This was also true for the *historia* of Friday. But even for those days that did have a wealth of material in the common repertory, sometimes inspiration was the maid of new creation.

An important trait that sets the Cantus sororum apart from other offices for the Blessed Virgin or for saints, is that, with the exception of hymns, the texts of the chants are neither rhymed nor metrical. Thus the Cantus sororum is not in the category of rhymed or metrical offices. Instead we are dealing with prose texts, sometimes with assonance and grammatical rhymes. Nor does the Cantus sororum have the characteristic modal order of the rhymed office, where the first chant is in the first mode, the second in the second mode etc. As the Cantus sororum can not be called an 'ordinary' office, it is possible to speak of a mixed form, a 'collage'.[18]

22 of the antiphons are borrowed and 12 are adaptations, i.e. new texts to existing melodies. As many as 55 antiphons are, so far, not known outside the Bridgettine order and can with a high degree of probability be ascribed to master Petrus. Most of them are to be regarded as centonisations, i.e. joined together of already existing and known melodic formulae. In this group there is a small number of chants with such a distinctive melodic style that they can be regarded as original compositions.

Two antiphons cannot be filed into any of the categories mentioned. In one of them, *Angeli, archangeli* (Ex. 1), the first part belongs to the common repertory, whereas the second part in all probability is a new composition, considering the affinity of melody to other Bridgettine antiphons. The other antiphon, *Glorificamus te* (Ex. 2), has a well-known text, but a melody which has so far not been found outside the Cantus sororum.

The antiphons of master Petrus are distinguished by a wide melodic range (*ambitus*), and late medieval style of melody. A fine example of such a piece is the Benedictus antiphon of Thursday, *Latuit,* which is the longest of all the antiphons. The melody has a range of nine notes and therefore is not outside the framework of the first mode, but the melody shows characteristic late medieval traits such as phrase endings on d" (Ex. 3).

---

18 Milveden 1964, p. 128.

Angeli, archangeli, virtutes, potestates, principatus, dominaciones, throni, cherubin et seraphin regem celorum, pro virgine, quam sibi in reginam preelegit, collaudate, nos quoque ad ipsorum laudem dignos efficite.

Example 1

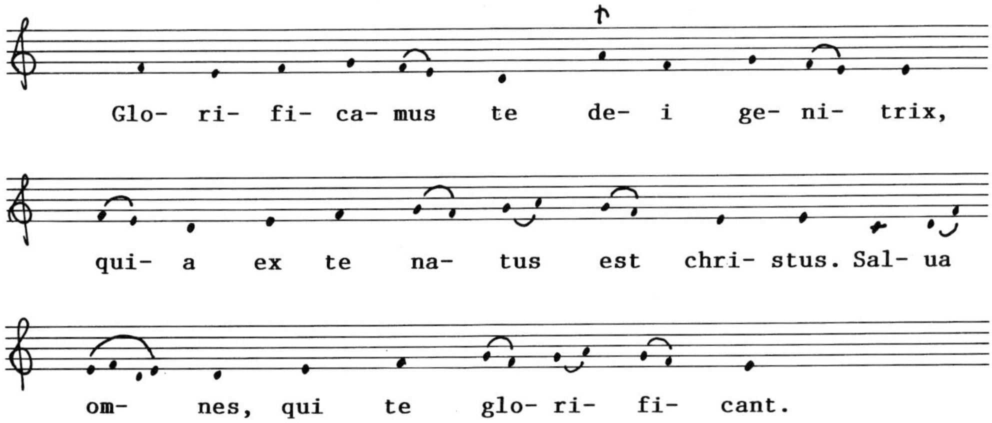

Glorificamus te dei genitrix, qui a ex te natus est christus. Salua omnes, qui te glorificant.

Example 2

Example 3

An example of a larger ambitus is the *Benedictus* antiphon of Tuesday, *Benedictus sis tu,* which has a range of 12—in some sources 13—notes. Here the modal framework is broken up and we pass on into *modus mixtus,* containing both first and second mode. The antiphon, incidentally one of the longest, starts in second mode:

Be- ne- dic- tus   sis tu, di- gnis-si-me   sa- tor

The melody continues in first mode:

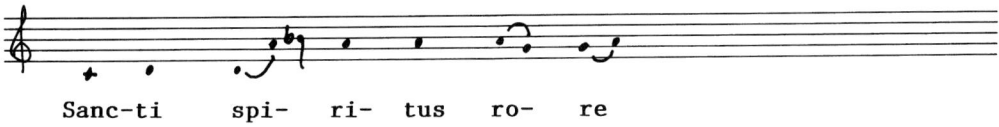

Sanc-ti   spi- ri- tus   ro-   re

After a while it progresses higher and obtains an ambitus of 12 notes:

quo re- fi- ci- un-   tur   an-   ge- li

In some variant sources the melody even climbs another step higher:

an-   ge- li

The opening of the vespers antiphon of Saturday *Iam letaris domina* is also in late medieval style. Here the downwards leap of a fifth, b–e, and then up again, e–b, attracts attention:

Iam   le- ta- ris do- mi- na nos- tra

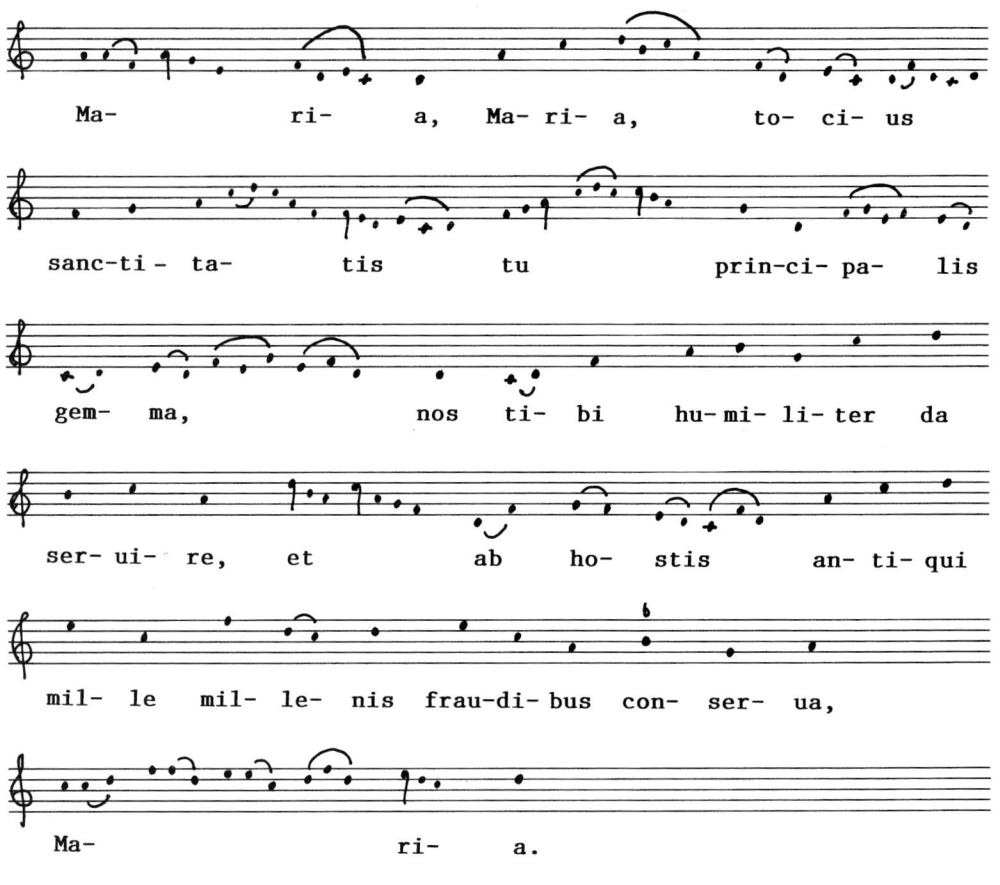

Example 4

Perhaps the most interesting and individual of all master Petrus' compositions is the *Magnificat* antiphon of Saturday, *Maria, Maria,* which starts in the first mode but has the psalm tone incipit in 8G (Ex. 4). This antiphon is of special interest as it contains, in all sources, an apparently unmotivated—and unsingable—leap of a fifth. By all accounts it seems to be a transposition in order to avoid the note E-flat, which at the time was not possible to notate. By the transposition of a fifth upwards at the place in question, the problem was avoided and the required semitone relation could be executed. If the melody is transposed down to its natural position it ends on the note G and can in a natural manner be linked with the psalm tone incipit:

With this antiphon we reach the concluding *Benedicamus Domino,* as the initium to *Maria, Maria* is found again in the Benedicamus trope of Wednesday (Ex. 5). This connection strengthens the hypothesis that these are original compositions.

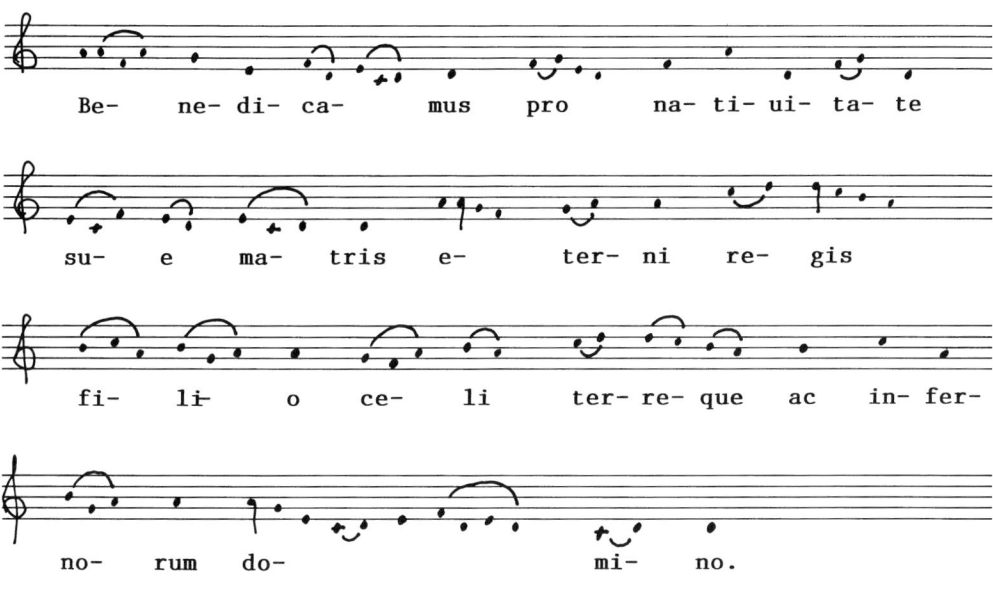

Example 5

The *Benedicamus* tropes are interesting in that they are as good as the only *Swedish* Benedicamus tropes within the art of troping. They occur in two series, one for ordinary days of the year and one for Easter. Altogether there are nine melodies. For all days except two the same melody is used in both series. The melodies for Sunday, Wednesday and Friday are not known outside the

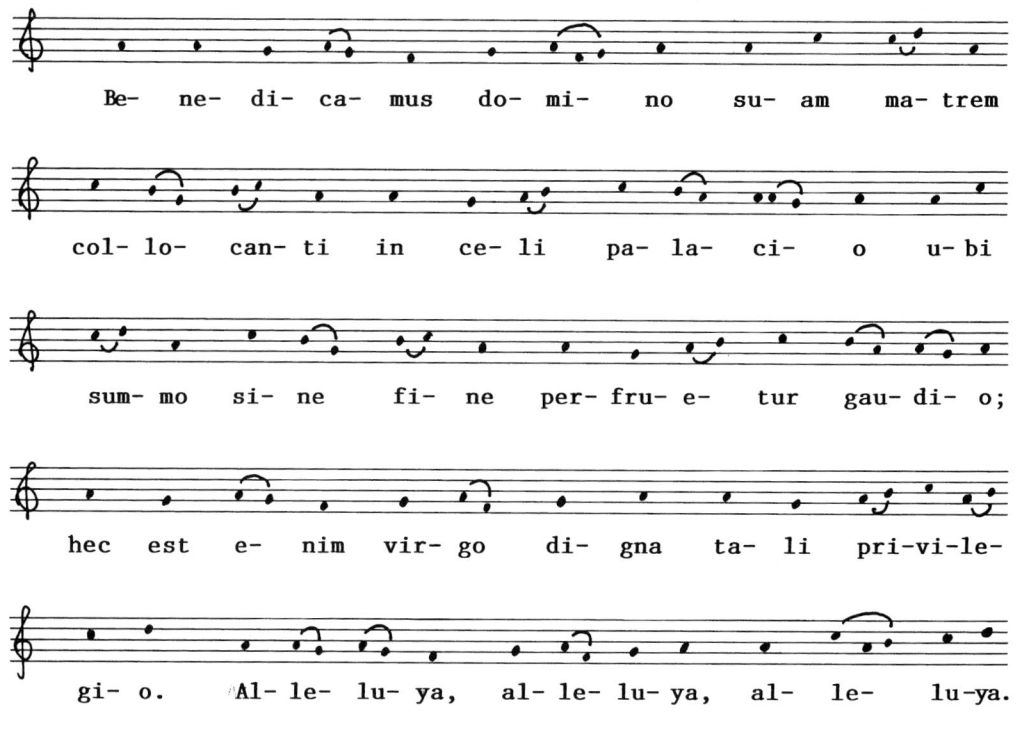

Example 6

Cantus sororum, whereas the melodies for Monday and Tuesday are from the common repertory. For both Thursday and Saturday two melodies occur. In both cases the ferial melodies are known and the paschal melodies are unknown. Apart from the already mentioned melody for Wednesday the paschal melody for Saturday is interesting with its two cadences, of which the *finalis* is d" (Ex. 6).

Finally, what did it sound like? Above all the rhythm is of interest. The originally differentiated rhythm of Gregorian chant was lost during the late Middle ages. The neumes, the early notational signs found above all in 10th century manuscripts—though not all—give indications for long and short notes that gradually were lost with the introduction of staff-notation from the 12th century and onwards. The decline of rhythmic differentiation probably started around the year 1000, perhaps even earlier. For this reason different ways of grouping notes in melismas in late medieval manuscripts—including the Bridgettine ones—are of no significance, and the well known research into the grouping of neumes, the 'coupures neumatiques' by Dom Eugène Cardine is not applicable.

We do not know how the process of rhythmic equalisation came about, for instance: Was there any difference at all between long and short notes? Could short ligatures be drawn together into quicker notes (ornaments), or did all notes become of equal length, allowing us to speak of equalistic rhythm? The influences from other genres of music are also of interest, as Gregorian chant sometimes in the late Middle ages was written in mensural notation, or at least something resembling mensural notation, which, indeed, is the case with some of the Bridgettine manuscripts from the Netherlands.

If rhythmic differentiation still did exist in the late medieval period, it is natural to assume that, as earlier, there where differences between different genres. It is appropriate to refer to Dom Cardine's assumption that chants with metrical texts had a metrically bound rhythm and chants with prose text had free rhythm.[19] Thus it is possible to assume that in later times hymns, sequences and metrical offices were still sung in metrically bound rhythm, whereas the originally differentiated rhythm of Gregorian chant became more and more equalistic, except in those cases where mensural notation crept in.

Possibly there were exceptions. We may ask if not only the textual structure, but also the *musical style and function* of the different chants influenced rhythm. With this reasoning the simple syllabic antiphons of the breviary that were sung by a large group, i.e. the whole convent, for practical reasons could have been performed in a more bound rhythm than e.g. the *introitus* of the *Schola* or the *graduale* of the soloist.[20]

In the final analysis the important thing was the spiritual attitude, the attitude that the chant was regarded as sung prayer, which is reflected in one of St. Bridget's revelations:

> The Son of God speaks: "Have you not read that Miriam, the sister of Moses, when God had helped the people across the Red sea, went out with virgins and women and with the accompaniment of drum and cymbal sang a chant of joy to God? So shall the daughters of my mother walk out of the red Sea, that is to leave behind greed and the lust to please this world, and they shall carry in their hands the drum of their deeds; a chant that must not be flaccid and weak, nor broken, nor sprightly, but refined and low and in unity and above all humble. They should strive to imitate the singing of the Carthusians. The chanting of these monks bear witness of their inner peace, humbleness and piety rather than of a lust to startle. For the soul is not free from sin when the singer finds more pleasure in the music than in the words that are sung and it is hateful before God when the voice is raised more for the sake of the listeners than for the sake of God."[21]

---

19 Cardine1963, p. 25.
20 The author is at present conducting a research project into Gregorian rhytm and semiology, in which these questions are being examined.
21 *Revelationes extravagantes,* chapter 4; ed. Hollman 1956, p. 118.

Bibliography

Cardine 1963 "Le chant grégorien est-il mesuré?", *Études grégoriennes* 6 (1963, p. 7–38).

Collins 1969 Collins, A. Jefferies, *The bridgettine breviary of Syon Abbey* (Worcester 1969).

Gejrot 1988 *Diarium Vadstenense. The memorial book of Vadstena Abbey. A critical edition with an introduction.* Diss. Acta universitatis Stockholmiensis. Studia Latina Stockholmiensia 33 (Stockholm 1988).

Hollman 1956 Hollman, Lennart (ed.), *Revelationes extravagantes.* Collections published by Svenska Fornskriftsällskapet, serie 2:5, (Uppsala 1956).

Huebner 1973 Huebner, Dietmar von, "Zu Prozessionen und Gesängen eines Processionale des 15. Jahrhunderts aus dem Birgittenorden", *Festschrift Altomünster 1973.* (Aichach 1973, p. 82–130).

Milveden 1964 "koral, Gregoriansk", *Kulturhistoriskt lexikon för nordisk medeltid* 9 (Malmö 1964, p. 116–129).

Nilsson 1991 *On liturgical hymn melodies in Sweden during the middle ages.* Diss. (Göteborg 1991).

Servatius 1977 Servatius, Viveca, *Benedicamustroperna i Cantus sororum.* 60-poängsuppsats; unpublished (Stockholms universitet 1977).

Servatius 1990:1 Servatius, Viveca, "Magister Petrus från Skänninge som "diktare" och "tonsättare" till Cantus sororum", Heliga Birgittas trakter. Nittion uppsatser om medeltida samhälle och kultur i Östergötland "Västanstång" (Uppsala 1990, p. 215–234).

Servatius 1990:2 Servatius, Viveca, *Cantus sororum. Musik- und liturgie-geschichtliche Studien zu den Antiphonen des birgittinischen Eigenrepertoires. Nebst 91 Transkriptionen.* Diss. Acta Universitatis Upsaliensis. Studia musicologica Upsaliensia. Nova series 12 (Uppsala 1990).

Office Antiphons in the First Mode: Context, Structure, Development and Aesthetics, with Examples of a Working Method

Eva Rungwald

The Office and the Antiphon

Before looking at the antiphon in a musical and structural context, it may be profitable to have a look at some early testimonies of Christian worship and the terms: antiphon and antiphonal singing.

In AD 313, Constantine the Great allowed Christianity as a religion in the Roman Empire, and in 381 it was made the official state religion. These events marked the start of Christian monasticism. As fervent Christians no longer found ways to holiness through martyrdom, many went out into the Egyptian desert to pray and fast, and having learned the 150 Psalms of David by heart they recited them[1] day and night[2]. The monks lived isolated from one another, though soon it became a tradition to come together on the night between Saturday and Sunday in order to recite the psalms together. They divided into two groups and sang the verses: *antiphonein*[3]. The response then took the name of *antiphon*.

Basil the Great (c. 330–379), who is considered to be one of the founders of eastern monasticism, writes in one of his letters: *Among us the people go at night to the house of prayer, and, in distress, affliction, and continual tears, making confession to God, at last rise from their prayers and begin to sing psalms. And now, divided into two parts, they sing antiphonally with one an-*

---

1 Jones, Cheslyn *The Study of Liturgy*, New York 1992, p. 405, The concept of constant prayer was in itself nothing new; what was new was the monastic understanding of it ... the invention of *recitatio continua*, the practise of reciting the whole Psalter, in its biblical numerical order, over a given period of time and number of offices, without any reference to the hour, the day, or the season.
2 Tertullian († after 220) expresses this when he says:*Pray always, everywhere and at all places. Opera pars II, De jejunio, Corpus Christianorum, Series Latina*, Turnholti 1954, p. 1267. Semper et ubique et omni loco orandum.
3 From the Greek αντι "anti" (in return) and "phone" φωνη (sound): meaning two choirs in turn singing against each other.

other, thus at once confirming their study of the Gospels and at the same time producing for themselves a heedful temper and a heart free from distraction.[4] Three main stages in the development of singing the Psalms of the Office should be mentioned:

Singing *In directum* meaning without refrain. The solo singer recites the psalm from beginning to end.[5]

Responsorial singing, where the assembly answers the first singer with acclamations such as *Halleluja* and *Amen*. St. Augustine (354–430) gives evidence of this practise, when he writes: *The Psalm which we have just responded to with our voices, is short, and very profitable*[6]:

Example of a Responsorial Psalm

Verse		**Refrain**
Solo		All
V. 1 Benedicam	*Dominum	R. In omni tempore[7]
V. 2 Semper laus eius	*in ore meo	R. In omni tempore
V. 3 Gloria Patri et Filio	*et Spiritui Sancto	R. In omni tempore
V. 4 Benedicam	* Dominum	R. In omni tempore[8]

And the *Antiphonal singing*, where two choirs sing a psalm against one another each choir singing a verse in return. In the beginning the antiphon was sung by all between each verse[9]:

Example of Psalmody with Two Choirs Alternating

1st cantor	*1st choir*
1 Attendite popule meus doctrinam meam[10]	Alleluia
2nd cantor	*2nd choir*
2. Inclinate aurem vestram in verba oris mei	Alleluia
1st cantor	
3. Quanta audivimus … etc.[11]	

---

4   Schaff, P. & Wace, H. (eds.), *The Nicene and Post-Nicene Fathers*, vol VIII, Basil: Letters and select works, p. 247, Peabody Massachusetts 1995. For the original greek text with latin translation see Opera, *Patrologiæ Graecæ* (Turnholti (without date)), vol 32, column 763.3.
5   The tractus' of the Mass is a trace of this practise.
6   One of the most famous examples is to be found in St. Augustin (AD 354–430), in his Commentary to the Book of Psalms, *Enarrationes in psalmos* 119.1, Aurelii Augustini Opera pars X, 3 Corpus Christianorum, Series Latina XL, Turnholti 1956, p. 1776, 1. *Breuis psalmus est et ualde utilis, quem modo nobis cantatum audiuimus et cantando respondimus.*
7   Psalm 34.1 I will bless the Lord at all times: his praise shall continually be in my mouth.
8   Responsorium breve *Benedicam, Antiphonale Monasticum* p.157.
9   The invitatorium has retained this musical form with repetition of the antiphon between the verses.
10 Psalm 78.1 Give ear, O my people, to my law: incline your ears to the word of my mouth.
11 *Graduale simplex*, Rome 1975, p.204.

Later it became the practice only to sing the antiphon before and after the psalm.

The female pilgrim Egeria gives an interesting testimony of antiphons and the singing of psalms in her descriptions of the liturgy in Jerusalem, a site she visited between the years AD 381–384. She states the hours observed and their structure and content as for instance concerning the office of Vigils on Sunday: *But on the seventh day, the Lord's Day, there gather in the courtyard before cock-crow all the people ... those who are afraid they may not arrive in time for cock-crow come early, and sit waiting there singing hymns and antiphons, and they have prayers between ... Soon the first cock crows, and at that the bishop enters, and goes into the cave of Anastasis ... when they are inside, a psalm is said by one of the presbyters; with everyone responding, and it is followed by a prayer, then a psalm is said by one of the deacons, and another prayer; then a third psalm is said by one of the clergy, a third prayer, and the Commemoration of all ... all the monazontes (monks) go back into the Anastasis to sing psalms and antiphons until daybreak. There are prayers between all these psalms and antiphons.*[12] And about the Lucernare (Vespers): *For some time they have the Lucernare psalms and antiphons ...* [13].

The antiphons, which seem in the beginning to have been very short (the ferial antiphons), became larger and more developed, especially the antiphons for the canticles Benedictus and Magnificat.

Sometimes musical settings of prose texts were called antiphons without the function of being a prelude and a postlude to the recitation of a psalm or a canticle, for instance the big antiphon for the Blessed Virgin Mary, concluding the office of Compline, is an individual through-composed piece. The antiphons of the mass[14], however, have kept the musical form: refrain-verse-refrain seemingly connected to the recitation of psalms.

---

12 Wilkinson, John (ed.), *Egeria's Travels to the Holy Land,* Jerusalem 1981, pp. 124–125, 24.8–9 & 12, Maraval, Pierre (ed.) Égérie Journal de voyage (Itinéraire), Sources Chrétiennes no 296, Paris 1982, pp. 242–244, 24.8–9 & 12, *Septima autem die, id est dominica die, ante pullorum cantum colliget se omnis multitudo ... Dum enim uerentur, ne ad pullorum cantum non occurrant, antecessus ueniunt et ibi sedent. Et dicuntur umni nec non et antiphonae, et fiunt orationes cata singulos ymnos uel antiphonos ... Mox autem primus pullus cantauerit, statim descendet episcopus et intrat intro spelincam ad Anastasim ... Quemadmodum engressus fuerit populus, dicet psalmum quicumque de presbyteris et respondent omnes, post hoc fit oratio. Item dicit psalmum quicumque de diaconibus, similiter fit oratio, dicitur et tertius psalmus a quocumque clerico, fit et tertio oratio et commemoratio omnium ... Iam ex illa hora reuertuntur omnes monazontes ad Anastasim et psalmi dicuntur et antiphonae usque ad lucem et cata singulos psalmos uel antiphonas fit oratio.*
13 Wilkinson, *Egeria's Travels to the Holy Land*, pp. 23, 24.4 Maraval, Pierre (ed.) Égérie Journal de voyage (Itinéraire), Paris 1982, p.238, *Dicuntur etiam psalmi lucernares, sed et antiphonae diutius.*
14 Introit, Offertory and Communion.

I find the table on the next page useful to demonstrate how even the catholic Vespers of today have preserved and incorporated the various liturgical elements from the early Middle Ages and to see the antiphons in a general liturgical context.

Roughly spoken, one can say that the left column is based on the testimony of Tertullian[15] and the right one on the testimony of Benedict of Nursia[16].

A satisfying explanation of the terms Cathedral and Monastic offices and other aspects of early liturgical history would be too complex to be dealt with within the limits of this article[17].

Office Antiphons in the First Mode

The present study takes it point of departure in my master's thesis[18], which was concerned with showing important features in the evolution of antiphons in the first mode through an investigation of first hand antiphons from the *Hartker Antiphonarium*.

There are about 1500 antiphons in different modes found in most medieval manuscripts[19]. Both the high number of antiphons and their well defined phraseology provide relevant material for comparative studies.

Also the fact that many of these antiphons were (and still are) used in Benedictine monasteries and consequently are part of a living liturgical practise made the study even more relevant to me.

For practical reasons only antiphons found in Antiphonale Monasticum were studied. The study entailed a detailed comparison of musical formulas and the structures in word and music. By comparing the antiphons and by referring to a number of different manuscript versions of some of the antiphons, it was

---

15 Tertullian (ca 160–222) *De Anima* IX,4: *Iam vero prout Scripturæ leguntur, aut psalmi canuntur aut allocutiones proferuntur aut petitiones delegantur.* Eventually they read the Scriptures, or sing Psalms, or give instruction or say prayers.
16 The Rule of St. Benedict (c. 530) is the first document that in detail describes the eight Office Hours and in detail distributes the 150 Psalms on hours and weekdays. (Chapter 8–20).
17 The following books can be recommended: Bradshaw, Paul *The Search for the Origins of Christian Worship*, Cambridge 1992, Bradshaw, Paul *Two Ways of Praying*, Nashville 1995, Claire, Jean "Le répertoire grégorien de l'office. Structure musicale et formes", Extraits des Actes du Colloque International de Musicologie. Louvain 1980, and Saulnier, Daniel *Le chant grégorien, quelques jalons*, Fontevraud 1996.
18 Rungwald, Eva "Les antiennes du premier mode; leur structure, évolution et esthétique", University of Copenhagen (unpublished master's thesis) 1989.
19 Hiley, David *Western plainchant. A Handbook,* Oxford 1993, p. 89.

The Origins of the Office: Vespers

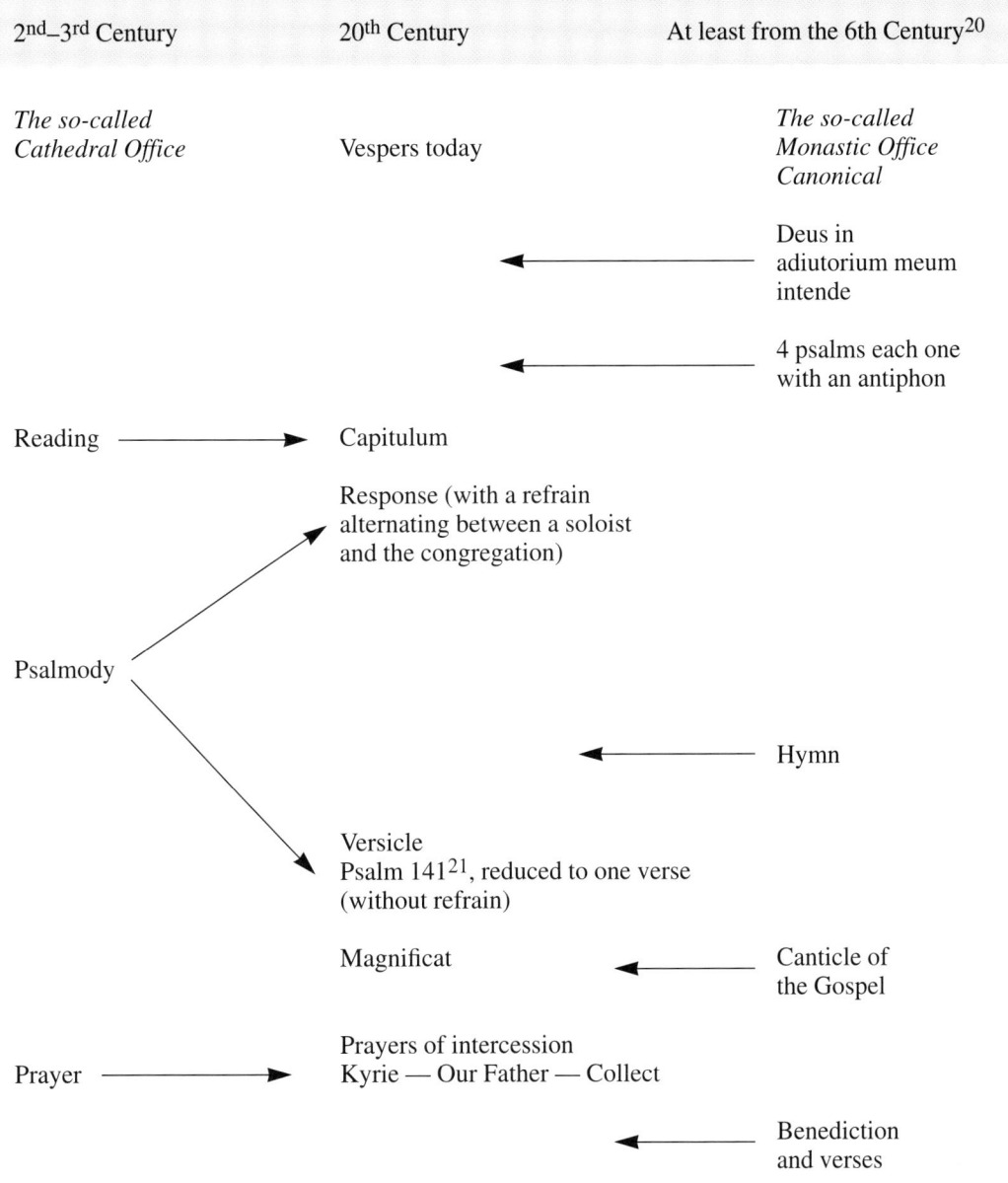

20 In chapter 13 of *Regula Sancti Benedicti* Benedict says about the cantica of Lauds that it is *according to the tradition in the Roman Church, sicut psallit Ecclesia Romana*. Unfortunately there is not written evidence of the Roman rite, but it surely existed before the Rule of St. Benedict, and Benedict has drawn upon it when writing his Rule.

21 Wilkinson, *Egeria's Travels,* p. 56. … we know from other sources that a psalm in general use at the morning office was Psalm 63 (Deus, Deus meus es tu) and that Psalm 141 (Voce mea ad Dominum clamo) was a regular constituent of the office held in the evening.

hoped that at least a minor contribution could be made to the next edition of *Antiphonale Romanum.* This is currently under preparation at St. Peter of Solesmes, (France). It was further hoped that the wider knowledge of textual and modal structures presented could be of use in future work in questions pertaining to the restoring of manuscripts.

Some of the conclusions from my master's thesis can be summarised as follows:

1) The verbal-modal character[22] of the chant was reconfirmed.
2) The importance of certain tones in the first mode was demonstrated. Also the use of B and B flat above the 6th step of the scale was accounted for.
3) Examples were given showing the function of the quilisma signaling a minor third.
4) Examples were given of the scandicus-quilisma[23] sign used to express notes of interrogation in the text.
5) A presentation of liturgical periods where certain problems in the adaptation of melodies to new texts seem to occur was given.

The Comparison of Antiphons

Below is a brief outline of the working methods which I learned at St. Peter of Solesmes, the famous Benedictine abbey south-west of Paris, where the Gregorian chant has been studied without interruption since 1850. The material for my investigation is taken from the oldest source of the repertoire of the office: *Codex Hartker*[24] (St. Gallen cod. 390–91), dating from around the year AD 1000. This manuscript was the main source of the repertoire in the *Antiphonale Monasticum*[25]. Antiphons from another and later hand can also be found in *Codex Hartker*. However, those antiphons have not been included in my studies. Excluding the latter, there are 215 antiphons of the first mode left for a thorough examination.

---

22 The chant formula is verbal because it is constructed on the basis of words according to their accentuation. There is at least one accent prior to the ending of the formula. The formula is modal because its function normally is to link up the final note with the recitation note. In the first mode for example the final steps of the four formulas are a (la), g (sol), f (fa) d (re), forming a nice curve and showing at the same time the secondary recitation notes of the mode.
23 One of the Gregorian signs still under discussion in recent scholarship.
24 The scribe Hartker, who in the illumination of codex 390, p. 11 presents himself offering his book to Saint Gall, was a monk and priest at St. Gall. In 980 he retreated to *cella sancti Georgii,* where he lived as a recluse until his death on December 21st 1011.
25 *Antiphonale Monasticum pro diurnis horis* no. 818 F, Tournai 1934, (henceforth A.M.).

The methods used in my thesis were influenced by the studies of Dom Ferretti[26]. However, without the works on semiology by Dom Eugene Cardine[27] and those of his students[28] the research would not have been possible.

The studies were made with the help of "La Paléographie Musicale" at St. Peter of Solesmes, and especially Dom Jean Claire[29], who was conducting the choir and was the leader of *La Paléographie Musicale* for 25 years (from 1971–95). He taught me the working methods, and provided me with the materials necessary for the studies.

My first step was to divide the antiphons into two main groups: the timbres and the centons.

A *timbre* (also called melody-type) is a standard melody, which has been used for several texts with only small alterations to fit it to the text, its accents and its length. The adaptation, however, does not change the main structure of the melody. A timbre melody can be divided into units, normally referred to as formulas. In a timbre melody the order of the formulas is always the same. The term timbre is used parallel with the term melody-type in recent works on Gregorian chant[30].

A *centon* melody consists of different melodic fragments combined to new melodies. The expression refers to the cloak of the roman legionary: a *centon*, because it was made of many (a hundred!) pieces of various sizes and materials.

The timbres and the centons found in the first mode almost exhaust the antiphons of the Hartker Antiphonary. There are, however, a few antiphons that do not fit into either category[31]

Ferretti[32] uses only the designation *mélodie-type*. The method of Ferretti was to divide the melody-types into sections and classify all the sections of

---

26 Ferretti, Paulo *Esthétique grégorienne*, Paris-Tournai-Rome 1938.
27 Cardine, Eugène *Sémiologie grégorienne*, Extraits des *Études Grégorienne XI*, Solesmes 1970. Cardine, Eugène *Gregorian Semiology*, Solesmes 1982. English translation by Robert M. Fowels.
28 Agustoni, Luigi *Gregorianischer Choral*, Freiburg 1963.
   Turco, Alberto *Il canto gregoriano*, vols 1–2, Roma 1987.
29 Claire, Jean "Les formes musicales de l'office romano-bénédictin", *Actes du Colloque S. Benoît, Louvain 1980*, pp. 27–50. and *Les répertoires liturgiques latins avant l'octoéchos. I. L'office férial romano-franc*, *Études Grégoriennes XV*, 1975, pp. 5–192.
30 For example the definition in Madrignac, André G. & Pistone, Danièle, *Le chant grégorien*, Paris 1984, p.122. Mélodie-type: dite également timbre. Mélodie adaptée á plusieurs textes littéraires, par de légéres modifications n'altérant pas sa structure.
31 Between the antiphons of timbres and the antiphons of centonisation there are two longer formulas each used for only two antiphons. They are referred to as semi-timbres. These formulas have not passed on into centonisation. Similary of the 215 antiphons of the first mode there is only one antiphon which contains formulas neither from the timbre nor from the centonisation: *Gratias tibi Deus* A.M. 534 from the Feast of the Holy Trinity.
32 Ferretti, *Esthétique grégorienne*, p. 92.

melody-types together with the sections of the centonised antiphons. This is possible because almost all the formulas from the timbres are also found in the centonisation. But Ferretti's method makes it impossible to observe the historic stratification of the composition, and this was one of my focal points: first the timbres and secondly the centons. I did not divide the timbre-melodies, but I classified them and compared them with each other, leaving out phrases from the centonisation.

In my research I have found indications that the timbres constitute the older part of the repertoire of antiphons and the centons the younger part.

In the oral culture of the early Middle Ages, where words and music were not yet written down but learned by heart, it must have been important to economise on what to learn. What would have been considered a good melody might well serve many other texts. The idea of originality, as it is known today, did not exist. Furthermore, it is known from the history of the liturgy that the temporal part of the office is older than the sanctoral[33], and it is here that most of the timbres are to be found. This is the case for all modes, not only the first mode.

The Timbres

In the first mode, also called authentic protus, I found three timbres[34]. Below is presented the first timbre, which I consider to be the most interesting. It is a big timbre and therefore especially good for studies of musical treatment of accentuation, phrasing and the treatment of liquescence[35]. The timbre consists of 30 antiphons. Twenty of these[36] can be analysed as follows, and the remaining ten are quite similar[37].

---

33 Martimort, A.G. *L'Église en prière. Introduction à la Liturgie*, IV *La liturgie et le temps*, Tournai 1983, "Le Culte des Saints" p. 124–139.
34 Rungwald, "Les antiennes du premier mode, leur structure, évolution et esthéthique", pp. 8–19.
35 Cardine, *Gregorian Semiology, p.215. Liquescence is a vocal phenomenon caused by the articulation of a complex combination of syllables. This requires the vocal organs to momentarily assume a position which diminishes or impedes the sound.*
36 The 1st timbre: Page numbers refer to: A.M.

Antequam convenirent	191	A		B	F	Z
Beati pacifici	623	A		B	F	Z
Clarifica me	398,406	A		B	F	Z2
Cum facis	334	A		D	f	Z3
Cum immundus	364	A		B	F ( )	Z
De quinque panibus	374	A		B	F	Z2
Deposuit potentes	158	A	( )	B	F	Z1

A/a — B/D — F/f — Z/Z1/Z2/Z3

A	represents the first formula of the timbre.
a	phrase **a** is a short version of formula **A**, used because of a very short text. It is a quite commun formula in the centons.
B/D [38]	represents the second formula of the timbre.
F	represents the third formula of the timbre.
f	phrase **f** is a short version of formula **F**, used because of a very short text.
Z/Z1/Z2/Z3	cadence formulas of the timbre.

36 (Continued)

Ecce nomen Domini	186	A	( )	B	F		Z2
Ecce puer meus	256	A		B	F		Z1
Ecce veniet desideratus	227	A		B	F		Z3/Z
Euge serve … in modico	670	A		B	F		Z
Herodes iratus	260	A		B	F		Z2
Joannes vocabitur	924	A		B	F		Z1
Qui me confessus fuerit	640	A		B	F		Z1
Qui mihi ministrat	640	A		B	F	( )	Z
Qui vult venire	644,737	A		B	F		Z1
Sunt de hic stantibus	256	A		B	F	( )	Z
Tradetur enim gentibus	358	A		B	F		Z3
Transeunte Domino	329	A		B	F		Z1
Tu autem	335	A		D	F		Z3

The brackets indicate that more music has been added, probably because of a longer text or in order to express something special.

37 Antiphons somewhat different to those above but still close to the 1st timbre; free space has been left when the phrase varies fundamentally.

Coenantibus autem	434	A			F		Z2
Corpora Sanctorum	648,938	A			F		Z1
Cum accepisset	444	A		D	F		Z3
Dum conturbata	441	A		D	F		
Dum esset summus	663,741,826	A			F		Z
Ex utero	921	A		B			Z
Hoc est testimonium	224	A			F		Z2
Qui me sanum fecit	350	A			F		Z
Qui verbum Dei	322,325	A			F		Z
Secundum multitudem	326	A			F	( )	Z

38 The reason for not using the letter C is that this letter was reserved for the cadence formulas of the centon melodies.

Melodic Table of the First Timbre

The second formula has two different melodies: D ends on d (re), and B ends on g (so). Finally, one can observe the beginning of centons with several possibilities for the fourth formula, the cadence formula (Z, Z1, Z2, Z3).

The antiphon *Antequam* A.M. 191 is sung at Benedictus of the Lauds Tuesday in the first week of Advent: *But before they lived together she was found to be with child from the The Holy Spirit*, (Mat.1.18b):

Closer examination of the first formula, A, shows that it is indeed verbal-modal[39]. Following the prosthesis[40] the main word with the accent is *convenírent*. A *pes quadratus* expresses the importance of the main accent on the syllable -*ní*. The recitation tone and the final step of the formula is the same: a (la), this very modal step which is of first importance to the first mode.

Formula B takes the melody from a (la) to g (so), secondary recitation tone. Again, the main accent is treated with great care. The second syllable of the name *María* is treated with a *pes quadratus* and a letter of elevation: a[41]. The accent on -*ven* is set in relief by the melody with an elevation to B flat. There is no doubt of the authenticity of the B flat. One will find the same formula in antiphons where the semitone is fixed e-f (mi-fa)[42].

The formula F also recites on g (so), but it uses the lower part of the scale under g (so). Here the principal accent is treated with a *virga strata*. The formula finds its rest on f (fa).

In the final phrase Z, there is a redundancy in the music because of the *alleluia*. Here again a diminished liquescence is used.

Looking at the antiphon as a unit one can see that it is based on the structural notes of the first mode. The first formula (A) takes us to the recitation note a (la). The second formula (B) brings us to g (so), which is the recitation note of the mode protus quarte[43] (Then formula F, the third formula of the timbre, after

---

39 See above, note 21. I also refer to: Jeanneteau, Jean "Style verbal et modalité", Revue Grégorienne 36, Paris 1957, p. 117, Jeanneteau, Jean "Los modos gregorianos", Studia Silensia XI, Silos 1985 and Jeanneteau, Jean & Saulnier, Daniel "Les fondements de l'analyse grégorienne", Études Grégoriennes XXIV, Solesmes 1992 p.46 *Le grand-oeuvre de la composition grégorienne s'accomplit dans la symbiose du mot et du mode. Qui dit "symbiose", dit "vivre ensemble". La vie du texte et la vie du mode ne deviennent plus séparables, et l'expression reçue de "contrepoint verbal-modal" est encore insuffisante. Puisqu'en latin, l'intelligibilité du mot ne s'atteint que sur l'ultime syllabe, c'est aussi sur la finale des mots que se décide l'intelligibilité de la mélodie. Les travaux de monsieur le chanoine Jeanneteau ont depuis longtemps montré comment l'architecture de la pièce se construit par la déposition du mouvement rythmique sur les finales de mots, tandis que, selon une expression audacieuse, l'accent chante "hors-modalité". Une fois connue cette loi de la composition, l'analyse des pièces grégoriennes se mène sur deux fronts simultanement: le texte et la mélodie. Concrètement, le parametre relationnel de la verbo-modalité nous aide à distinguer dans les pièces les cellules mélodico-verbales. Pédagogiquement, on peut dire que chaque mot ou locution verbale est équipé de sa mélodie.* (In the semi-ornamented style).
40 Initial part of the formula leading to the principal accent of the phrase.
41 Cardine, *Gregorian Semiology*, p. 224.
42 For example, A.M. 163 *Suscepit Deus* (7th mode).
43 The expression derives from the specific medieval terms for the eight modes; *protus* authentus (1st mode), *protus* plagis (2nd mode), *deuterus* authentus (3rd mode) etc. The *protus quartus* is a modern name given in extension to medieval terminology. It is a mode with finalis on d (re) that recites on the fourth step of the scale: g (so). In modern books of chant as *Liber hymnarius* and *Psalterium monasticum* such melodies have been given the designation: 2*. See also *Psalterium Monasticum*, Solesmes 1981, p. ix.

reciting on g (so) goes to f (fa), which is a secondary recitation note of the first mode. The familiarity with the second mode is so obvious here, with f (fa) beeing the recitation note of the Protus Plagal (The second mode). The cadence formula Z brings the formula to rest on the finalis d (re). The structural notes a (la) g (so) f (fa) and d (re) form in themselves a harmonic curve, and they may be called archetypal for the first mode.

The next table indicates the placement of the tonic accent and shows how it is treated:

First Mode, First Timbre, First Formula: A and its Minimum a

Looking once again at the antiphon *Antequam*, now in the comparative table, it can be seen that the word with the tonic accent is *convenírent*: the syllable with the acute accent is a paroxytone (an accent on the next to the last syllable of a word ex. Déus.)[44]. The paroxytone is treated with a *pes quadratus* and the ac-

---

44 Crouan, Denis *Le chant grégorien son esprit sa pratique*, Montsûrs 1987, pp.17–18 *D'après la place de la syllabe accentuée, les mots latins peuvent être classés en trois catégories: lorsque l'accent est mis sur une syllabe finale, on dit que l'on a une cadence* oxytonique *(le mot en question est un* oxyton*). En fait, ce cas ne se présente que dans les monosyllabes placés en fin de phrase: … sequatur* **me**. *(Le mot me étant ici placé en fin de phrase, il est accentué). Lorsque l'accent est sur l'avant-dernière syllabe d'un mot, on dit que la cadence est* paroxytonique *(le mot en question est un* paroxyton*): … sequatur* **Deum**. *Enfin, l'accent placé sur l'avant-dernière syllabe d'un mot donne une cadence* proparoxytonique *(le mot est un* proparoxyton*): … sequatur* **Dominum**.

cent receives the notes f-a (fa-la). The note a (la) is an anticipation of the final note a (la) which is the tenor. Futher down, there are examples of the way the composers treat the proparoxytones (a accent on the antepenultimate syllable ex. Dóminus), and of the phenomena of liquesence, which has to do with the influence of certain consonants on the duration and sonority of the note[45]. All the other formulas of the timbre have been analysed using similar methods of comparison.

The Centons

The centons differ from the timbres in the way that the formulas of a centon melody can be borrowed from the timbres, from other centon melodies or invented for the purpose of a new text. Then they are joined together in a new musical pattern.

A centon uses phrases from the timbres, but the classical order of the formulas is not necessarily respected and the timbre formulas are mixed with centon formulas. In the centons there are various ways of using the musical material. There are, for example, cadences used as initial formulas, something that would never occur in a timbre.

Tradent enim[46] A.M. 621 (at Magnificat at Apostle Feasts[47]) begins with formulas close to the first timbre, then finishes on a cadence often used in the centons; begins again with the first formula of the second timbre (Ba), and contin-

---

45 Cardine, *Gregorian Semiology*, pp. 215–223.
46 They will put you before the council and into the synagogues and scourge you before kings and magistrates because of me so that you may bear witness for them and for the nations. Conf. Mat.10, 17–18.
47 Extra tempus pascali.

ues with a second formula from the first timbre (D). There are also two middle formulas (M14 and M8) from the centon repertoire ending up with the formula C7. One extra phrase appears that, in my research, does not occur elsewhere. It seems to be unique, and has not been given a letter.

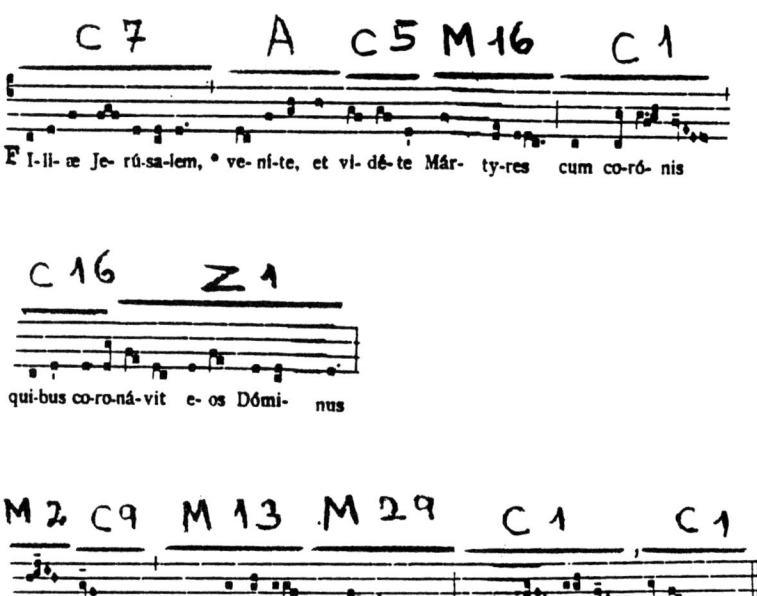

Filiæ Jerusalem[48] A.M. 636 (at Benedictus, at Feasts for Apostles and Martyrs at Easter) begins with a cadence, and eight of the musical formulas used here are cadences from either the timbres or the centons. Both antiphons are to be found in the Sanctoral (Commune Apostolorum).

When studying the timbres, one experiences the harmony between the formulas and their inner life, which submits to the accentuation of each phrase. As for the centons, the use of formulas and their linking is more free. There is a tendency, that the centons contain more formulas and use more of the modes recitation tones. On feasts that are of a later date, several examples can be found of centons which exemplify both irregularities in the accentuation and in the use of formulas. Apparently, the linking of formulas is not made with the same ease

---

48 Daughters of Jerusalem come and see the martyrs with the crowns that the Lord crowned them with on this day of celebration and joy.

as in the older repertoire, and the general rules of how to apply a text to a melody are followed less the further away one comes from the timbres.

Finally, I present a table conserning the development of the first mode. This is partly based on research by Dom Jean Claire notably the research conserning archaic composition of Gregorian chant[49]. The table presents the development of the first mode:

The Development of the Antiphons in the First Mode

	Intonation	Tenor	Cadence	A.M
Archaic composition	0	on a (la) and g (so)	on a (la) with Bb:	139
Elementary composition	from d (re) to a (la) = formula A	on a (la) and g (so) = formula M9	from a (la) to d (re) = formula Z	66 366b
Stage of evolution	formula A	formula M15 + M9	Z inconclusive + Z definitive	107
1st timbre	formula A	formula B+F	Z	50

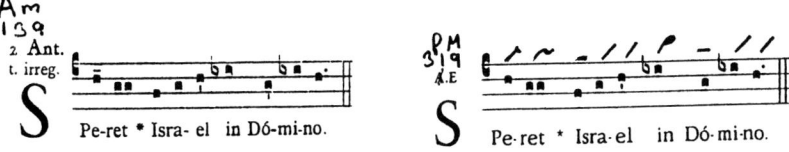

The example of archaic composition *Speret Israel in Domino*[51] A.M. 139 (2nd ferial antiphon at Vespers on Tuesday) is marked in A.M as t. irreg., but with the discovery of the archaic modes C, D and E, the mode of this antiphon is now called: E[52]. In the archaic modes the tenor coincides with the final[53].

---

49 Claire, Jean "L'évolution modale dans les répertoires liturgiques Occidentaux", *Revue Grégorienne 40*, 1962, pp. 196–211 & pp. 229–245. and Claire, Jean "Les répertoires liturgiques avant l'octoéchos.I. L'office férial romano-franc", *Études Grégoriennes XV*, Solesmes 1975.
50 Conf. pp. 8–13, **The timbres**.
51 Let Israel hope in the Lord.
52 *Psalterium Monasticum*, (henceforth P.M.), p.x and p. 319.
53 More information on this field of modality is found in: Saulnier, Daniel *Le chant gregorien, quelques jalons, pp. 40–50, D'Antimi, Fausto Antologia pour l'initiation à l'étude du chant grégorien à l'usage des conservatoires, Solesmes 1994, pp. 62–114 and Madrignac & Pistone, Le chant grégorien, p. 63–64.*

About this field of research Dom Jean Claire says:

> In the last 30 years our knowledge of Gregorian modality has improved considerably. The system of eight church modes, or octoechos, traditionally taught since the time of the Carolingian theorists, has been severely criticised, but with constructive results. Today they are not considered as the obligatory starting point for all studies on the subject, but rather as the end of a long evolution. It is merely the system, a little forced, of a repertoire that has developed in different locations, becoming better known ... As a matter of fact one must start with the cantillation in order to explain the song. The development of recitation on the three cordes-mères[54]: C, D, E, decorated according to the taste of the soloist has given birth to the melodies of the Gradual and the Antiphonal, both concerning the modal structure and the ornamentation (melismas)[55].

Here follow some examples of elementary composition. In *Jesus autem*[56], A.M. 366b (at Magnificat, Monday in the third week of Lent), the formula M9 a-g a-g (la-so la-so) is a sign of the "corde-mère" E (MI)[57], which is basic to the first mode. M9 is a formula used frequently (66 times in the 215 antiphons studied in my thesis).

54 As for terms to use David Hiley suggests *tonal matrix* in English and *Ur-ton* in German (personal communication). In Danish I have until now used the terms *arkaisk tone* or *urtone*.
55 Turco, Alberto *Il canto gregoriano*, Roma 1992, preface. (My translation from French).
56 But he, passing through the midst of them, went his way. (Luc. 4.30).
57 Claire, Jean "L'évolution modale dans les répertoires liturgiques occidentaux", *Revue Grégorienne 40*, 1962, pp. 229–245.

In *Spiritu principali*[58] A.M. 66 (1st ferial antiphon, at Lauds Friday), *Codex Hartker* indicates only one note at <u>con-</u> but various other manuscripts[59] give the augmentative liquescence which may indicate a-g (la-so).

The characteristics of the formula M15 are that from the tone of recitation, it goes to b natural, returns to the chord of recitation, turns around g (so) and finds its rest on a (la).

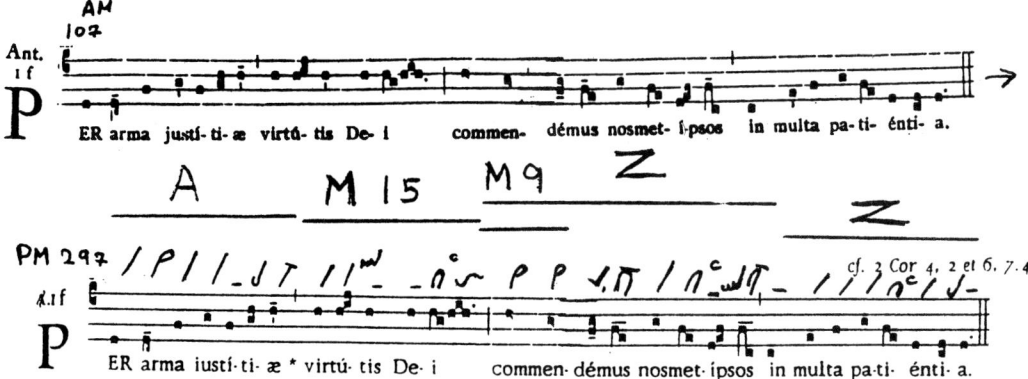

In *Per arma justitiæ*[60] A.M. 107 (None on Mondays in Lent), the melody even goes to c (do) on the second syllable of the word virtútis with a *scandicus-quilisma*.

In contrast to the research of Ferretti[61] my studies try to approach the historical development as it can be observed by studying at first the timbres and then the centons. In the timbres one can see the well-balanced organisation and the inner life of the antiphon depending on the different accentuation. In the centonisation one can observe a more free linking together of formulas, though very often inspired by the timbre, using its various formulas of intonation, middle-formulas and cadences. One can also see how the rules for adaption between text and melody are observed less and less the further away you get from the timbre. There is also in the centons a tendency towards using more and longer phrases, a larger ambitus of the melody and the use of more tones than in the timbres.

---

58 Confirm my heart, oh God, with the Spirit of Force.
59 The most important being: Codex Lucca 602, Paléographie Musicale, tome IX and Codex Worcester 60, folio 35, Paléographie Musicale, tome XII, but also Piacenza 65, folio 303, Paris Bibliothèque Nationale, lat 12044, Silos and Karlsruhe LX.
60 By the armour of righteousness and the force of God, we will try to improve ourselves in much patience.
61 Ferretti, *Esthétique grégorienne*, pp. 86–124.

Bibliography

Agustoni, Luigi *Gregorianisher Choral,* Freiburg 1963.

Alfonso, P. *L'Antiphonaire dell'Ufficio Romano,* Subiaco 1935.

Antiphonale Missarum ambrosien, Rome 1935.

Antiphonale Monasticum pro diurnis horis no 818, Tournai 1934.

Antiphonaire de Hartker, Codex Saint-Gall 390–391, Solesmes 1992.

Apel, Willy *Gregorian Chant*, Bloomington 1958.

Augustin, Aurelius *Opera pars X, 3, Corpus Christianorum, Series Latina 40*, Turnholti 1956.

Basilius, S.N.P. *Opera, Patrologiae Graecae, tomus 32*, Turnholti (without date).

Bradshaw, Paul *The Search for the Origins of Christian Worship*, Cambridge 1992.

Bradshaw, Paul *Two Ways of Praying*, Nashville 1995.

Cardine, Eugène "Cadences oxytoniques et cadences rompues", *Revue Grégorienne 25*, 1946, 71–78, 99–106.

Cardine, Eugène *Sémiologie Grégorienne*, Extraits des *Études Grégoriennes XI*, Solesmes 1970. English translation by Robert M. Fowels, *Gregorian Semiology*, Solesmes 1982.

Cardine, Eugène *Vue d'ensemble sur le chant grégorien*, Extraits des *Études Grégoriennes XVI*, Solesmes 1977.

Cattin, Giulio *Music of the Middle Ages I,* Cambridge 1984.

Claire, Jean "Antiennes et tons psalmodiques", *Revue Grégorienne 41*, 1963, pp. 49–62, 77–102.

Claire, Jean "L'évolution modale dans les répertoires liturgiques Occidentaux", *Revue Grégorienne 40*, 1962, pp. 196–211 & pp. 229–245.

Claire, Jean "Les formes formes musicales de l'office romano-bénédictin", *Actes du Colloque S. Benoît*, Louvain 1980.

Claire, Jean *Les répertoires liturgiques avant l'octoéchos.I. L'office férial romano-franc*, *Études Grégoriennes XV*, Solesmes 1975.

Corbin, Solange *L'Église à la conquête de sa musique*, Paris 1960.

Crouan, Denis *Le chant Grégorien son esprit sa pratique*, Montsûrs 1987.

D'Antimi, Fausto *Antologia pour l'initiation à l'étude du chant grégorien à l'usage des conservatoires*, Solesmes 1994.

Ferretti, Paulo *Esthétique grégorienne*, Paris-Tournai-Rome 1938.

Graduale Simplex, Rome 1975.

Hesbert, R.J. *Corpus antiphonarium officii*, Rome 1979.

Hiley, David *Western Plainchant a Handbook*, Oxford 1993.

Jeanneteau, Jean "Style verbal et modalité", *Revue Grégorienne 36,* Paris 1957.

Jeanneteau, Jean *Los modos gregorianos, Studia Silensia XI*, Silos 1985.

Jeanneteau, Jean & Saulnier, Daniel "Les fondements de l'analyse grégorienne", *Études Grégoriennes XXIV*, Solesmes 1992.

Jones, Cheslyn *The Study of Liturgy*, New York 1993.

Liber hymnarius, Solesmes 1983.

Madrignac, André G. & Pistone Danièle *Le chant grégorien Historique et pratique*, Paris 1984.

Maraval, Pierre *Égérie journal de voyage (Itinéraire), Sources Chrétiennes no 296*, Paris 1982.

Martimort, Aimé-Georges (ed.) *L'Église en prière: Introduction à la liturgie, vol. IV, La liturgie et le temps,* Tournai 1983.

Psalterium Monasticum, Solesmes 1981.

The Rule of St. Benedict in Latin and English with notes, Collegeville 1981.

Rungwald, Eva "Les antiennes du premier mode; leur structure, évolution et esthétique", University of Copenhagen (unpublished master's thesis) 1989.

Saulnier, Daniel *Le chant grégorien,* Solesmes 1995.

Saulnier, Daniel *Les modes grégoriens,* Solesmes 1997.

Schaff, P. & Wace, H. (eds.) *The Nicene and Post-Nicene Fathers*, vol VIII, Basil: Letters and select works, Peabody Massachusetts 1995.

Taft, Robert F. *The Liturgy of the Hours in East and West*, Collegeville 1986.

Tertullian, Quintus S.F. *Opera pars II, De jejunio, Corpus Christianorum, Series Latina 2*, Turnholti 1954.

Turco, Alberto *Il canto gregoriano*, vols 1–2, Roma 1987.

Turco, Alberto *Traccie di struttura arcaica nelle antifone del Temporale e Santorale*, Milano 1972.

Wilkinson, John (ed.) *Egeria's Travels,* Jerusalem 1981.

Understanding Medieval Chant and Liturgy

Nils Holger Petersen

Introduction

In recent years the general interest in the Middle Ages has also brought with it a gradually increased public interest in Gregorian Chant separated from its liturgical use. In the Nordic countries—marked by a strong Protestant tradition—this is a remarkable development which partly seems to be connected to existing tendencies towards a new ritualism and more generally with a modern longing for unified artistic spiritual experiences in the midst of a complex and—also esthetically—bewildering culture.

In this paper I will take up some hermeneutical issues concerning this so-called Gregorian Chant and the rituals to which this chant belonged. The increasing interest in and practical work with the performance of medieval liturgical music and the reconstruction—to some degree—of its original contexts has made it an important task to raise the consciousness of what we are doing when we try to approach such distant rituals. This, of course, can be done for different reasons and—accordingly—with very different attitudes. For the devout Catholic the search for the medieval origin of current liturgical practices is a very different venture from the above-mentioned detached cultural quests of a Protestant or an agnostic member of a modern secularized society.

In both cases, however, the rituals and the music focussed upon are distant cultural phenomena, cultural utterances that grew out of historical circumstances radically different from ours. It is important to realize that it is our modern interests, arising from our lives in the present cultural environment, which lead us to an interest in the old medieval practices—whether we are conscious of it or not. This is crucial since the less conscious we are of our own motives the less we will be able to separate these from the medieval objects we are trying to study. The study of medieval liturgy has to some extent been marked by such anachronistic prejudices—either from the points of view of the reform Catholicism as expressed in the Council of Trent and the liturgies (*Missale Roma-*

num 1568 and *Breviarium Romanum* 1570) resulting from it or from the opposite, yet very similar prevalent attitudes of particularly scholars of medieval literature and drama until not very long ago.[1]

The aim of this paper is to demonstate the fruitfulness of the *new historicism* concept of *alterity* for the study of and concerning the attitudes towards the reconstruction of (parts of) the medieval liturgy. The work of scholars like C. Clifford Flanigan, Rainer Warning and Johann Drumbl in the last decades has indeed been informed by such a hermeneutical approach, otherwise not commonly found in liturgiological scholarship.[2] The following discussion will reflect the work of these scholars at the same time as it tries to incorporate the inter-arts aspect of the medieval liturgy to a higher degree than has been done so far.

Preliminaries and Hermeneutical Remarks

As my point of departure I will quote certain key formulations by the German literary scholar, Hans-Robert Jauss, who has discussed the hermeneutics of medieval literature. Using the concept of *alterity* he has drawn attention to the otherness of this literature and the new possibilities it gives for a different approach to the Western literary tradition on the whole, which since the Middle Ages overwhelmingly became a written and work-focused tradition.[3]

Jauss summarized his hermeneutical program in the following words:

> Put in the briefest possible manner, it is a new attempt to discover the modernity of medieval literature in its alterity.[4]

Here *modernity* does not signify the idea that one should be able to find contemporary positions or discussions reflected in medieval texts. On the contrary:

> ... modernity means the recognition of a significance in medieval literature which is only to be obtained by a reflective passage through its alterity.[5]

---

1   See Flanigan 1996, pp. 15–16, and Hardison 1965, essay 1, on the anti-clericalism in the works of E.K. Chambers and the evolutionism in both his, Karl Young's and other scholars' works on medieval liturgy.
2   Flanigan 1986; Flanigan 1996; Drumbl 1984; Warning 1979.
3   Jauss 1979, p. 182: ... *I propose to justify the research and educational interest in medieval literature on three grounds: the aesthetic pleasure, the surprising otherness, and the model character of medieval texts.* Compare also ibid, p. 187.
4   Jauss 1979, p. 198.
5   Jauss 1979, p. 198.

The significance of medieval literature in other words is seen by Jauss as its ability to throw modern attitudes, ways of living, and art forms into relief through its alterity.

Similar considerations apply to the medieval liturgy and music to a considerable extent. When Gregorian Chant is performed in concerts or in excerpts from the original liturgical context as it is most often done—for practical but, I believe, also for other reasons—new contexts are created leading to new meanings and new experiences. This is perfectly legitimate, but precisely necessitates the mentioned *reflective passage through the alterity* of the historical Gregorian phenomena.

Indeed, historical reconstructions are different in this respect, since they represent a different level of historical inquiry. But, in fact, the problematic remains. When arranging or participating in a reconstruction, no matter how exact it could possibly be—and, of course, it can never fully be—it still remains a modern reconstruction since we are not living in the Middle Ages and therefore the context is totally different. A "medieval" office or procession reconstructed in our age is a different cultural event than the "same" event in the historical cultural practice it imitates. A similar approach to ancient practices would have been unthinkable in the Middle Ages, the idea of a reconstruction belongs to the modern world just as our interest in history does.[6]

No matter how much we try, it is not possible to become historically innocent so that we for instance could listen to the Gregorian Chant freed from later concepts or ideas culled from the history of esthetics, such as "art works" or "originality".

The Gregorian Chant must, in other words, be understood through its function and significance in its contemporary liturgical setting as well as through the history of its reception, the consequences of which basically can be said to be the whole history of musical composition. The Gregorian Chant is marked by an alterity which must be taken as an important part of its modern appreciation, but it must at the same time be recognized that the chant is an integrated part of, or rather the point of departure for the history of Western musical composition as well. This is probably the reason why we can more easily appreciate the music than the original ritual settings. In the last section of this paper I will give a reading of a particular example of a medieval ritual where the verbal as well as the musical text seems to underline the alterity of the ceremony, the distance to a modern liturgical thinking.

---

6   Compare Petersen 1996, pp. 126–27. Concerning the medieval use of the historical past, see Häussling 1973, pp. 104–5 also discussed in Petersen 1995 pp. 213–15.

Gregorian Chant

The so-called Gregorian Chant as a historical cultural phenomenon cannot meaningfully be studied from a musical angle alone. The study must involve both the music itself, the words of the liturgy, and the ritual practices to which it belongs, as well as a general understanding of the theological and cultural background for such practices. The Gregorian Chant thus naturally becomes a subject for what in recent years has been termed *interarts studies*, a humanistic discourse dealing with cultural manifestations in ways that cannot be contained within the individual traditional disciplines of the arts.

In this paper I will not introduce the general scholarship which presently is evolving within this discourse.[7] Rather, I will integrate an interarts aspect by involving various media in my interpretations.

Historically, the Gregorian Chant is not a totally well-defined corpus of songs. The myth that the chants of the medieval liturgy were composed or put together by pope Gregory the Great around the year 600, from which myth the chant received its still current name has been replaced in modern scholarship by much more complicated theories of the process of its making—as it is well known. Among the many variants suggested by 20th-century scholarship the probably most widely accepted today refers the "composition" or rather the finalizing of an archetype of the proper chants of the Mass antiphonary—the first corpus to actually get to a point where one can postulate the existence of such an archetype—to the Royal monasteries of the Carolingian Kingdom or Empire around 800; (the earliest preserved fully notated Mass antiphonaries stem from the end of the 9th century). Many of the proper chants, however, were still in a process of change during the following century and the fixed corpus of both proper and ordinary songs still took some few hundred years to be established.[8]

---

7   Generally, very little has been done in terms of combining liturgical studies and interarts scholarship. However, I have dealt with this theme in Petersen 1996 as well as in two forthcoming studies Petersen 1997 and Petersen forthcoming, "Les textes polyvalents …". There I give short introductions to interarts studies. For a historical and terminological introduction see Clüver 1993.
8   In general I refer to Hiley 1993/1995 for a modern updated introduction to the study of medieval Western chant. Concerning the question of oral and written transmissions of the Western chants there are differing opinions. Kenneth Levy has argued for the existence of a written archetype for the Gregorian chant already at the time of Charlemagne (768–814). On the other hand, Helmut Hucke and Leo Treitler have worked out the probably most influential recent hypothesis according to which an oral transmission of the Gregorian chant went on continuously into the eleventh century (alongside the existence of manuscripts from c. 900). For presentations of the main points of these authors see: Hucke 1980; Treitler 1981; Levy 1987. See also Jeffery 1992, pp. 11–50, and Hiley 1993/95, pp. 520–21.

Thus the corpus of the Gregorian Chant is not easily if at all separable as a corpus of musical composition from what was described for many years as a somewhat later corpus of Frankish additions to the official Mass and Office liturgy of for instance tropes and other proses and—not least—sequences. I am not trying to imply that there is no way of making distinctions between the established musico-literary canon of the Mass and—to a lesser degree—the Office chants on the one hand and, on the other hand, the less fixed and vast output of poetico-theological or musico-literary additions to the established canon. But I am saying that as a compositional endeavour it is not possible to distinguish between two clearly separated time periods or groups of creative craftsmen behind the two types of musical items. Thus the two terms Gregorian and Frankish Chant cannot be clearly separated as it has been stated by Richard Crocker, among others.[9]

What remains of the original historical myths of the import of a Roman chant to the Carolingian realm in the 8th and 9th centuries is a complicated model of a Carolingian interest in shaping the liturgical chants, also musically. In terms of their verbal texts these chants were to a large extent—but even in this respect not exclusively—of a Roman origin. The musical "composition" was based on Roman melodies but also to an unknown degree on Gallican local traditions and on new composition.

Combining the traditional liturgical and church historical scholarship with musicology and other art disciplines such as theatre history and art history, has provided an astonishing—although far from finished—picture of a rich and complicated ritual constituting a symbol of the unity of the Sacred Carolingian Empire as well as a combination of the idea of the City of God with the notion of the terrestrial life of the Christian community walking together towards eternity in the processional liturgy which developed in the Carolingian monasteries, based on the Roman stational liturgy, on Roman verbal texts, on Roman melodic material to some extent, but certainly in all these cases using astonishing amounts of re-interpretations and of new ideas combined with the traditions in-

---

9   See Crocker 1990, pp. 227 and 243, and Hiley 1993/95, pp. 518–19. Concerning the different status of the Mass antiphonary and the tropes (and other chants) see Planchart 1988, esp. pp. 218–19 and 245.
    Trope scholarship in general is quite comprehensive. In addition to the account in Hiley 1993/95, pp. 172–286, I will refer to the long-standing Stockholm project concerned with text-critical editions of trope texts, the *Corpus Troporum* which has led to a number of important publications by Ritva Jacobsson, Gunilla Iversen and Gunilla Björkvall since 1975. The latest volume in the series is Andrews Johansson 1998. The music has only been dealt with occasionally. Further volumes are forthcoming.
    Concerning the music of the tropes I further refer to Crocker 1990; van Deusen 1989, Rankin 1994, esp. pp. 303–313. For editions of introit tropes, see Weiss 1970.

voked.[10] Both the particular Carolingian way of employing the traditions—of quoting the past—and the contemporaneous theologico-cultural ideas involved are very remote, indeed, from even the most ritualistic mind of our days.

In the following I will discuss a rogation ceremony from the Norwegian liturgical use of Nidaros.

The Order for the Rogation Processions in the Province of Nidaros

The three rogation days were placed immediately before Ascension, i.e. ending on the Vigil of Ascension. The following description is derived from the *Ordo Nidrosiensis* composed in the early decades of the 13th century[11] in the edition of Lilli Gjerløw.

The Mass of the day follows upon Sext and is again followed by a procession.[12] After Mass the shrine of the blessed martyr Olav is put on a bier and the

---

10 See the interpretations in Häussling 1973 (as further elucidated below at n. 23). Cf. also Petersen forthcoming, "Quem quaeritis ..." where the processional liturgy of the Carolingians is discussed in the light of Häussling's account and through the theologico-philosophical interpretations of the concept of time in the *Confessions* of St. Augustine.

11 Gjerløw 1968; concerning the dating esp. pp. 38 and 73.
The edition was almost exclusively based on Icelandic manuscripts, the earliest of these dating from the thirteenth and fourteenth centuries. Only one fragment of the *Ordo Nidrosiensis* (in the sequel *ON*) from Norway is part of the edition. *Ibid.* p. 58, 61, 64, 68, 70, 71, 72. Concerning the lack of Norwegian sources see pp. 33–34.

12 ... *Missa uero completa, dum scrinium beati martiris Olaui deponitur et depositum in feretro collocatur, cantetur responsorium* **Sancte olaue** *cum versu et* **Gloria patri** *et sequatur versus* **Ora pro nobis beate olaue** *cum oratione* **Propiciare nobis domine quesumus**. *Post orationem uero statim incipiatur antiphona* **Exurge domine** *cum psalmo* **Deus auribus** *et* **Gloria patri** *ebdomedario subinferente versum* **Ostende nobis** *et orationem* **Mentem familie tue quesumus domine intercedente beato olauo martyre tuo, et interim aqua benedicta aspergatur et sanctorum reliquias portaturi ordinentur et ordinatis illis reliquie collocantur. Et imposita antiphona* **Surgite sancti** *sic cantando exeat processio et eundo ad ecclesiam in qua missa de letania dicenda est cantetur autem antiphona prefata cum ceteris antiphonis rogationum quotquot prolixitas itineris permiserit et cantoribus uisum fuerit cum .vij. psalmis penitentialibus et antiphona* **Ne reminiscaris domine**. *Cumque ecclesie quam adituri sunt appropinquauerint, responsorium de sancto loci imponatur et cum versu suo et* **Gloria patri**, *si opus fuerit, in ecclesia finiatur. Quo finito versus cum oratione de sancto loci subiungatur vel officium* **Exaudiuit de templo** *statim inchoetur et unum tantum* **Alleluia** *cantetur. Missa quidem finita et reliquiis sanctorum sublatis letania* **Kirieleison. Christeleison. Domine miserere** *imponatur et sic eam decantando reuertantur. Cumque reuersi fuerint, reliquiarum portitores in loco suo eas deponentes genua flectant, letania uero interim prolongetur ut conuentus in chorum ueniret et reliquie sanctorum in loco suo collocate fuerint cessante signorum pulsatione. Antiphona de sanctis, id est* **Lux perpetua**, *imponatur. V.* **Exultabunt sancti** *et oratio* **Via sanctorum domini ihesu christi** *tonaliter subiungatur.*

Ordo iste processionalis per omnia seruetur in tribus diebus rogationum excepto quod in singulis diebus mutantur letanie et antiphone. Processione completa statim nona cantetur.

Gjerløw 1968, pp. 249–50. Compare the very similar procession for the *Letania maior* (April 25th) pp. 333–34.

respond *Sancte Olaue* is sung with its verse and the *Gloria patri*.[13] Then follows other songs and prayers involving Saint Olav.[14] Meanwhile holy water is sprinkled, the relics brought in order and as the antiphon *Surgite sancti*[15] is intoned the procession starts towards the church where what is here called the Mass of the Litany will be sung. The *ON* also mentions the singing of other rogation antiphons depending on the length of the walk and the judgement of the cantors, as well as the seven penitential psalms with the antiphon *Ne reminiscaris domine*.[16]

When approaching the church towards which the procession is headed, a respond of a saint of the place is intoned, ending—if necessary—with its verse and the *Gloria patri* in the church. Thereafter a verse and a prayer for the saint of the place is undertaken whereafter the Mass of the litany begins.[17] When the Mass is finished and the relics have been shown the Kyrie *Kirieleison. Christeleison. Domine miserere* is begun and as this is sung the procession returns. Upon the return the relics are put back in place (under genuflection). Meanwhile

---

13 *Sancte Olaue christi martyr* according to the *letania maior* of the *ON*. Neither the verbal nor the musical text is available in the *ON* nor in the published texts of the Nidaros antiphonary (in the following termed *AN*) edited in Gjerløw 1979.

14 Compare the order for the rogation processions in the important and influential tenth-century Roman-Germanic Pontifical (henceforth *PRG*). See Vogel and Elze 1963–72, vol. II, pp. 119–20. The prayer *Mentem familie ...* is found here as well as in the Gregorian Sacramentary (here for the *laetania maior*). See Lietzmann 1921, p. 64 (and similarly Deshusses, 1971–79, I, p. 211, noting a slight textual difference). In the Gregorian Sacramentary the stational church is specified as Sanctus Laurentius in Lucinae, hence the intercession (both here and in *PRG*) is different from the *ON*:

   Mentem familiae tuae, quaesumus, domine, intercedente beato Laurentio martire tuo, et munere, conpunctionis operi et largitate pietatis exaudi. Per.
   (We pray for a good will towards your family, Lord, through the intercession of your blessed martyr Lawrence, and hear us through the gift of the deed of compunction and the largeness of piety).

15 See again Vogel and Elze 1963–72, vol. II, p. 120:
   Surgite, sancti, de mansionibus vestris, loca sanctificate, plebem benedicite et nos homines peccantes in pace custodite, alleluia. De Hierusalem exeunt reliquiae et salvatio de monte Syon, propterea protectio erit huic civitati et salvabitur propter David famulum eius, alleluia.
   (Rise, saints, from your houses, sanctify the places, bless the people and lead us sinful men in peace, alleluia. From Jerusalem relics go forth, from the mount Sion salvation, therefore there shall be protection for this city and it shall be saved for the sake of David his servant, alleluia).
   The antiphon is also given with its musical text (from a Sarum source) in Bailey 1971, p. 53, although divided up into two (musically strongly related) antiphons for resp. psalm 66 and 131, see below at n. 25. Both in *ON* and in *PRG* the antiphon seems to have been used as an independent item. It is not clear whether both parts of the antiphon were sung in the *ON*.

16 Hesbert 1963–79 vol. III, p. 347 (in a different context, however) listed as no. 3861 (in the following the items from Hesbert's editions of the antiphonaries are given as CAO plus the number):
   Ne reminiscaris, Domine, delicta mea vel parentum meorum, neque vindictam sumas de peccatis meis.
   (Do not remember my crimes, Lord, or those of my parents: and do not punish me for my sins).

17 Gjerløw 1968, pp. 246, 250, and 496–97.

the litany goes on and when all are gathered in the choir the bells stop ringing. The antiphon of the saints *Lux perpetua* is intoned with its verse *Exultabunt sancti*[18] and the prayer *Via sanctorum domini ihesu christi* is then chanted.

This processional order with some further details is carried out by all during the three rogation days, except that the litanies and the antiphons can be changed for each day. When the procession is finished None is immediately intoned. The processional movement as well as the musical and verbal texts all play an important role so integrated into the total meaning of the ceremony that it makes little sense to undertake an analysis of one of the involved media alone.[19]

However, we do not possess the complete verbal text, and neither do we have the musical text. And we certainly do not have the total choreographical 'text' or the particular churches with their architectural and pictorial contributions to the ceremony. All these 'texts' would for obvious reasons not be the same for the various places and the various repetitions of the rogation procession that would have occurred within the province of Nidaros. As it is, the best I can do is to make two observations on the 'text' as I know it:

1) The verbal text has substituted St. Olav for St. Laurentius in the prayer *Mentem familie tue ...*[20] This, of course, is not very surprising in the *ON*. On the other hand, as the procession approaches the church where the Mass of the litany is supposed to be held, the verbal text is very careful to leave the names of the actual church and the saints to be invoked open. Obviously, the text was supposed to be used in many places throughout the province of Nidaros. But they did not possess the shrine of St. Olav in other places than the Nidaros cathedral. Interestingly, virtually all the manuscripts compiled for the *ON* stem from Iceland. So even though there would have been relics connected with St. Olav in many places and certainly almost everywhere churches and statues consecrated to this important saint, the literal verbal text remains strange.

---

18 CAO 3653, Hesbert 1963–79 vol. III, p. 321:

> *Lux perpetua lucebit sanctis tuis Domine, alleluia, et aeternitas temporum, alleluia alleluia alleluia.*
>
> (The eternal light shall shine upon your saints, Lord, alleluia, also the eternity of all time, alleluia alleluia alleluia).
>
> The mentioned verse is not listed in connection with the *Lux perpetua* here, but as an independent verse, CAO 8068, ibid, vol. IV, p. 487:
>
> *Exsultabunt sancti in gloria.*
>
> (The saints shall rejoice in glory).

19 It is clearly an intermedia text (in the recently developed terminology of the interarts studies denoting a text using more than one medium in such a way that the media cannot meaningfully be separated). See Clüver 1993, p. 17–47 and Petersen 1998.

20 See above, n. 14.

At this point it is worth while remembering how Frankish liturgical manuscripts although in many respects deviating from Roman practices still faithfully transmitted local Roman names of stational churches; for instance in the early Mass antiphonals[21], but also other local material as in the *PRG* (from Mainz c. 950) where the description of the pope's meeting with the *notarius regionarius ... in loco qui dicitur Merulanas* has been preserved (from the—several hundred years earlier—Ordo I).[22] A way of understanding such features has been provided by the interpretations of Angelus A. Häussling concerning the Carolingian wish to have a "Roman" liturgical order. Häussling discusses this in the light of the frequently symbolic function of medieval quoting.[23] The seeming contradiction between the Carolingian interest in importing the Roman liturgy and the independence with which the same Carolingians apparently treated the imported material, as it for instance can be seen in the mentioned "Roman" manuscripts of the Frankish liturgy, is possibly clarified in this perspective as well.[24] Even when the "Romanity" was provided through quoting less significant or even absolutely irrelevant material, it must still have provided the manuscripts and the liturgy with a symbolic authority.

In the province of Nidaros it is no longer only Rome, but also the local metropolis, here Nidaros, that is reflected in a similar way. Whatever the processional route, which the manuscript is constructed to leave open, the church where the procession starts somehow must have been thought to represent the cathedral of Nidaros. Most likely any important relic of the stational church for the letania minor would have been substituted for the bier with the shrine of St. Olav. But *all* the compiled manuscripts still do note St. Olav and his shrine as if in Nidaros.

2) I will comment on the antiphon *Surgite sancti de mansionibus ...*[25]. Below follows the Sarum version of the melody. Of course, there is no way of knowing for sure whether the version sung in the churches of the *ON* corresponded in all details to this version.

The verbal text expresses the view laid out in general above. The saints are invoked to lead the Christians on their way. The procession is understood as

---

21 See Hesbert 1935, for instance pp. 100–107 where four out of the six edited manuscripts give (most of) the Roman stations for the Easter week. Compare Baldovin 1987, p. 156.
22 Vogel and Elze 1963–72, vol. II, pp. 114–15.
23 Häussling 1973, esp. pp. 99, 104–5, 170–71, 201–10, and 299–307.
24 See Petersen 1995, pp. 210–18, discussing the question of *why the Frankish clergy ... should want Roman rites at all if they were so content with their current Gallican liturgies ...* raised by McKitterick 1977, p. 128.
25 See above, n. 15.

a walk governed by sacred figures who can keep the people (*plebs* and *peccantes*) to the path that will lead them to salvation. The saints rise from their houses, i.e. from the church(es) visited. Thus the space of the procession is shown to be of importance: The saint(s) in question are implicated by the coming of the procession to the house in question. The linear path towards the next celebrational ceremony is thus not only a matter of a general understanding of the situation of the faithful on his way between ceremonies that can keep him to the right (and safe) path, but also has the function of making it possible to invoke the important figure(s) necessary to carry out the needed intercession.

The musical text corroborates this picture. The rather melismatic melody (in mode 7) may at first seem not to have a very strongly emphasized form. It seems to go up and down touching again and again its low point of departure, the final G and the F below this. On second thoughts, however, one notices that it builds up in several steps, gradually reaching higher notes, first the b on *sur-gi<u>te</u>*, then the c and d on *man<u>sio</u>nibus*, further on *<u>loca</u>* repeating the same notes in the reversed order d and c proceeding to *sanc<u>ti</u>ficate* where d e d are reached twice. This is the high point of the melody not exceeded even in the long alleluia melisma towards the end:

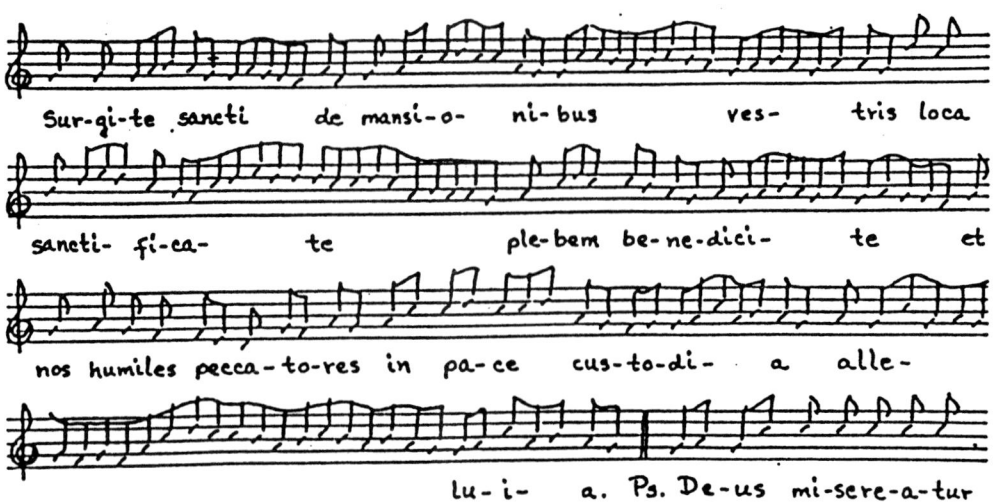

The upward extensions of the range seem to underline the following words: *surgite, mansionibus, loca sanctificate*. These are maybe not the words one would immediately think of as the most important ones in the verbal text.

From a modern perspective one might rather have pointed to the prayer for the blessing and the help on the way.

There is no contradiction, however, between the processional, verbal and musical text, but the music seems to stress the immediate purpose of the visit to the house(s) of the saints: the invocation of the saints in their houses. When that has been achieved the rest may have seemed to follow by itself. The ritual, it seems, was conceived in a more concretely efficacious way than what would be acceptable in a modern theological interpretation.

Sources

Andrews Johansson, Ann-Katrin, (ed.), *Corpus Troporum IX. Tropes for the Proper of the Mass 4. The Feast of the Blessed Virgin Mary* (Stockholm 1998).

Deshusses, Jean, (ed.), *Le Sacramentaire Grégorien. Ses principales formes d'après les anciens manuscrits I–II.* (Fribourg 1971–79).

Gjerløw, Lilli, (ed.), *Ordo Nidrosiensis Ecclesiae* (Oslo 1968).

Gjerløw, Lilli, (ed.), *Antiphonarium Nidrosiensis Ecclesiae* (Oslo 1979).

Hesbert, Renato-Joanne, (ed.), *Antifonale missarum sextuplex* (Bruxelles 1935).

Hesbert, Renato-Joanne, (ed.), *Corpus antiphonalium officium I–VI* (Roma 1963–79).

Lietzmann, Hans, (ed.), *Das Sacramentarium Gregorianum nach dem Aachener Urexemplar* (Münster in Westfalen 1921).

Vogel, Cyrille, et Elze, Reinhard, (eds.), *Le Pontifical Romano-germanique du dixième siècle I–III* (Citta del Vaticano 1963–72).

Weiss, Günther, (ed.), *Introitus-Tropen I. Monumenta Monodica Medii Aevi III* (Kassel 1970).

Other cited literature

Bailey, Terence, *The Processions of Sarum and the Western Church* (Toronto 1971).

Baldovin, John, F., *The Urban Character of Christian Worship* (Roma 1987).

Clüver, Claus, "Interartiella studier: en inledning", Lagerroth, Ulla-Britta, Lund, Hans, Luthersson, Peter, & Mortenson, Anders (eds.), *I Musernas Tjänst* (Stockholm 1993, pp.)

Crocker, Richard, "Medieval Chant" Crocker and Hiley, (eds.), *The New Oxford History of Music II: The Early Middle Ages to 1300* (Oxford 1990, pp. 225–309).

van Deusen, Nancy, *The Harp and the Soul* (Lewiston, N.Y. 1989).

Drumbl, Johann, *Fremde Texte* (Milano 1984).

Flanigan, C. Clifford, "Comparative Literature and the Study of Medieval Drama", *Yearbook of Comparative and General Literature* 35 1986 (pp. 56–104).

Flanigan, C. Clifford, "Medieval Liturgy and the Arts. Visitatio Sepulchri as Paradigm" Eva Louise Lillie and Nils Holger Petersen (eds.), *Liturgy and the Arts in the Middle Ages* (Copenhagen 1996, pp. 9–35).

Hardison, O.B, *Christian Rite and Christian Drama in the Middle Ages* (Baltimore 1965).

Häussling, Angelus A., *Mönchskonvent und Eucharistiefeier* (Münster, Westfalen 1973).

Hiley, David, *Western Plainchant. A Handbook* (Oxford 1993/1995).

Hucke, Helmut, "Towards a New Historical View of Gregorian Chant", *Journal of the American Musicological Society* 33 1980 (pp. 437–67).

Jauss, Hans Robert, "The Alterity and Modernity of Medieval Literature", *New Literary History* X, 2. (Charlottesville, Virginia 1979, pp. 181–229)

Jeffery, Peter, *Re-envisioning Past Musical Cultures* (Chicago 1992).

McKitterick, Rosamond, *The Frankish Church and the Carolingian Reforms 789–895* (London 1977).

Levy, Kenneth, "Charlemagne's Archetype of Gregorian Chant" *Journal of the American Musicological Society* 40 1987 (pp. 1–30).

Petersen, Nils Holger, "Synet på indførelsen af den romerske liturgi i Karolingerriget i nyere og nyeste forskning", *Dansk Teologisk Tidsskrift* 58 1995 (pp. 193–219).

Petersen, Nils Holger, "Liturgy and Musical Composition", *Studia Theologica* 50, 4 1996 (pp. 125–43).

Petersen, Nils Holger, "The Musical and Liturgical Composition of *Visitatio Sepulchri* Offices", Laszlo Dobszay and David Hiley, (eds.), *Cantus Planus. Papers Read at the 7th Meeting in Sopron, Hungary, Sept. 1995* (Budapest 1998, forthcoming).

Petersen, Nils Holger, "Quem quaeritis in sepulchro? The Visit to the Sepulchre and Easter Processions in *Piacenza 65*", Pierre Racine, (ed.), *Il Libro del Maestro. Codice 65 dell'archivio Capitolare della cattedrale di Piacenza (sec. XII). Atti del convegno Marzo 1997* (Piacenza, forthcoming).

Petersen, Nils Holger, "Les textes polyvalents du *Quem quaeritis* à Winchester au dixième siècle", Marie-Noël Colette, (ed.), *Le Drame Liturgique Médiéval* (Paris forthcoming).

Planchart, Alejandro E., "On the Nature of Transmission and Change in Trope Repertories", *Journal of the American Musicological Society* 41 1988 (pp. 215–49).

Rankin, Susan, "Carolingian Music", Rosamond McKitterick, (ed.), *Carolingian Culture: emulation and innovation* (Cambridge 1994, pp. 274–316), pp. 303–13.

Treitler, Leo, "Oral, Written, and Literate Process in the Transmission of Medieval Music", *Speculum* 56 1981 (pp. 471–91).

Warning, Rainer, "On the Alterity of Medieval Religious Drama", *New Literary History* X 1979 (pp. 265–92).

Aspekte der menschlichen und wissenschaftlichen Figur von Dom Eugène Cardine

Nino Albarosa

Fast zehn Jahre nach dem Tode von Dom Eugène Cardine habe ich die Ehre, in Trondheim über ihn zu sprechen. Eugène Cardine starb am 24. Januar 1988, fast 83 Jahre alt. Er war, wie bekannt, Benediktiner von Solesmes und Professor für Gregorianische Paläographie und Semiologie am Päpstlichen Institut für Kirchenmusik in Rom. Ich möchte seine Figur vor allem für diejenigen beleuchten, die das Glück nicht haben konnten, ihn persönlich kennenzulernen.

Eugène Cardine gehört zu der grossen gregorianischen Schule von Solesmes. Dom Jean Claire, sein berühmter Mitbruder, weist mit recht darauf hin, was uns nicht überrascht, dass der Gründer der gregorianischen Wissenschaft, die auf den alten Handschriften beruht, Dom André Mocquereau ist,[1] der aber mehr für sein Rhythmussystem bekannt ist als für die grossen Intuitionen in Bezug auf die Erforschung der alten neumatischen Handschriftenfamilien. Dies hat andererseits Dom Cardine in seinem Testament ohne weiteres zugegeben.[2]

Als er als 47-jähriger nach Rom kam, verfügte er über ein grosses Wissen und grosse Erfahrung. Mehr als er, der wenig über sich selbst schrieb, hilft uns noch einmal Jean Claire, der uns über sein Leben und seine gregorianische Tätigkeit reichlich informiert. Cardine überprüfte Diözesan- und Ordensproprien, um sie dem Stil der Vatikanischen Edition anzupassen, komponierte »neugregorianisch«, nahm auch an der Vorbereitung des *Antiphonale Monasticum* teil, und es gelang ihm, im 3. Psalmton das Si als Tenor neben dem Do einzuführen. Er wurde verantwortlich für den musikalischen Teil in der Arbeitsgruppe für die kritische Ausgabe des *Graduale Romanum* und besuchte mit

---

1   J. CLAIRE, *Dom Eugène Cardine*, »Études Grégoriennes«, XXIII, 1989, S. 18–19.
2   E. CARDINE, *Les limites de la Sémiologie en chant grégorien*, »Bollettino dell'Associazione Internazionale Studi di Canto Gregoriano«, X, 1985, S. 3–4; s.a. »Études Grégoriennes«, XXIII, 1989, S. 5.

Dom Jacques Hourlier die französischen Bibliotheken, um weitere Handschriften in seinem Vaterland zu finden.[3]

Wichtig war vor allem die Bearbeitung des auf den grossen Tafeln von Solesmes mit sanktgallischen Neumen über die der *Editio Vaticana* aufgebauten *Graduel Neumé*. Es ist anzunehmen, dass es schon aus dem Bedürfnis entstanden ist, den Gesang dem Geist der mittelalterlichen Zeichen anzunähern und damit aus dem Bestreben nach einer auf diesen Zeichen beruhenden Interpretation.

Mit seiner Ankunft in Rom beginnt die Zeit der grossen Beiträge, die ihn in aller Welt berühmt machen. Er überträgt Wärme und Sympathie, ist streng und ernst in der Methode, besitzt Mut und Klugheit, Phantasie und Vorsicht vor dem Irrtum. Er ist geduldig und grosszügig, begeistert und Gelehrter: daher entwickelt er seine wissenschaftlichen Thesen sowohl allein als auch, stufenweise, in Zusammenarbeit mit seinen Schülern.

Er war ein Mensch, der auf äusserliche typographische Mittel keinen grossen Wert legte. Seine Beiträge erschienen auch in einfachen Ausführungen, eventuell auch maschinengeschrieben. Das Gleiche gilt von seinen Vorträgen, die er bei grossen Kongressen oder vor einer bescheidenen Zuhörerschaft hielt.

Eugène Cardine gehörte zu jenen Menschen, die komplett sind. Er sagte gerne, dass das Wichtigste im Leben die *Synthese* sei. Und man kann sagen, dass er selbst eine Synthese war. Bei ihm ist es unmöglich, den Mönch vom Menschen und vom Gelehrten zu unterscheiden: er war immer Mönch, Mensch und Gelehrter zusammen. Seiner Abtei treu, kehrte er anlässlich jeder Unterbrechung des akademischen Jahres zu ihr zurück. Selbstverständlich widmete er den Schülern alle notwendige Zeit mit grosser Geduld, derer ich selbst Zeuge bin.

Drastisch in der Methode, aber auch im Leben: er schlief in der Nacht nur sechs Stunden und erklärte, sich nicht verzeihen zu können, eventuell sieben Stunden zu schlafen.

Als wir in der Benediktinerabtei Münsterschwarzach in Bayern für Gruppensitzungen zusammentrafen, verliess er, so wichtig das Diskussionsthema auch sein konnte, am Abend immer zur gleichen Zeit die Gruppe. Am Nachmittag spazierte er vor seinem Zimmer und las sein Brevier.

Zweimal durfte ich ihn zu Gast haben. Er kam nur, wie Solesmes vorschreibt, wenn dringende Anlässe es benötigten: in diesem Fall die zwei gregorianischen Kongresse, die 1977 und 1979 in Cremona organisiert wurden. Auch hier, fern von seinem Kloster, stand er immer um 5 Uhr auf und organisierte seinen Tag so gut wie möglich der monastischen Tagesordnung entsprechend.

---

3   J. CLAIRE, a.a.O. (Anm. 1), S. 15–16.

Bei den Treffen im Münsterschwarzach sprach er, auch wenn er weit mehr wusste als die anderen, nur wenn es notwendig war, und seine Persönlichkeit war auf keinen Fall »sperrig«. Immer diskret, immer achtungsvoll, gab er nur richtige Ratschläge.

In Luxemburg, während des Kongresses des Jahres 1984, des Kongresses der endgültigen Anerkennung, sass er ruhig und aufmerksam inmitten aller Zuhörer wie ein normaler Teilnehmer. Daher hat, zusammen mit anderen verständlichen Gründen, sein Tod eine grosse Leere geschaffen und, ehrlich gesagt, hat die europäische Gemeinschaft ihren Anhaltspunkt verloren und sich bis heute noch nicht erholt.

Was die Synthese seines römischen Aufenthaltes betrifft, kann man sagen, dass die besonderen Schwerpunkte die Frage des Prinzips der Neumentrennung,[4] die *Semiologia Gregoriana*[5] und der *Primo Anno di Canto Gregoriano* gewesen sind.[6]

Weniger bekannt, aber für ihn sehr wichtig, war auch die Frage der »unterschiedlichen Notenwerte«.[7] Natürlich sind auch andere Veröffentlichungen wichtig, unter denen möchte ich erwähnen: *Théoriciens et théoriciens. A propos de quelques exemples d'élision dans la mélodie grégorienne;*[8] *Paroles et mélodie dans le chant grégorien;*[9] *Le chant grégorien est-il mesuré?*,[10] berühmte Widerlegung der mensuralistischen Anschauung von Vollaerts und von dessen Anhänger Murray; wie auch der Aufsatz *Sur la modalité du chant grégorien*, wo er mit Autorität behauptet, dass die neumatische Schrift der *geschriebene* Leitfaden der Modalität eines Stückes ist.[11]

Über die Neumentrennung gibt es nichts Neues hinzuzufügen; vielleicht dass sie selbst eine gregorianische Welt bildet. Natürlich deckt sie nicht alle Bedürfnisse des »gesungenen Wortes«; trotzdem hebt sie, bei kleinen und grossen Melismen, sowohl für die Analyse als auch für den Rhythmus die kompositorischen Strukturen hervor.

---

4 Vgl. E. CARDINE, *Neumes et Rythme: les coupures neumatiques*, »Études Grégoriennes«, III, 1959, S. 145–154; ders., *Preuves paléographiques du principe des »coupures« dans les neumes*, »Études Grégoriennes«, IV, 1961, S. 43–54.
5 Roma, 1968.
6 Roma, 1970.
7 Vgl. E. CARDINE, *Nouveaux aspects sur l'interpretation du chant grégorien*, »Bollettino dell'Associazione Internazionale Studi di Canto Gregoriano«, II, 1977, 1, S. 10–15.
8 »Études Grégoriennes«, II, 1957, S. 27–35.
9 »Études Grégoriennes«, V, 1962, S. 15–21.
10 »Études Grégoriennes«, VI, 1963, S. 7–38.
11 »Bollettino dell'Associazione Internazionale Studi di Canto Gregoriano«, II, 1977, 2, S. 17–19.

Die Konsequenzen sind tief und enorm: und, wie Jean Claire wissen lässt, wäre es fehlerhaft, sie nur technisch zu betrachten und sie nicht im gesamten, auch kulturellen Wesen des gregorianischen Gesanges zu verankern.[12] Sicher steht sie in engem Verhältnis mit dem Text und dessen Akzentuierungen: ich möchte sagen, ist sie von dessen Akzentuierungen geleitet. Und selbst die Artikulationen in den grossen Melismen stellen Aspekte der »Verbalität«, der gesprochenen Sprache dar, während die Zeichen, wie allgemein in der Musik, den Grundwert, der ihnen eigen ist, nicht in anderer Weise angeben, als wenn sie, vor allem einzeln, direkt über dem Text stehen.

In Bezug auf den anderen Aspekt, der für Cardine wichtig war, nämlich die unterschiedenen Notenwerte, muss man sagen, dass er den der Neumentrennung ergänzt und ermöglicht, mehrere Möglichkeiten des Wertes der Einzelnoten zu bestimmen, die von den stark verkürzten, wie im Fall des Quilismas, bis zu den augmentierten gehen. Die Wertunterschiede, schreibt Cardine, »bilden distinkte und unter sich unterschiedene Werte, obwohl nicht genau messbar aufgrund ihrer natürlichen Ungenauigkeit. Hier finden wir uns mitten im *freien Rhythmus*. Diese ausserordentliche Nuanciertheit fällt von der Notenschrift der ältesten Handschriften ins Auge. Als Konsequenz ergibt sich: im Choral gab es ursprünglich nichts Systematisches, keinen 'theoretischen' oder 'ersten' absoluten Wert; alles war praktisch betrachtet: die Einheit der Silbe, die Silbe mittleren Gewichtes«.[13]

Wie sehr er von der Elastizität des gregorianischen Gesanges überzeugt war, kann man in seiner grossen Schrift, die sein Testament darstellt, lesen. Hier erzählt er, dass er einmal nicht wusste, wo er eine Stropha mit Episem zwischen syllabischem und augmentiertem Wert stellen sollte. So gab er dem fragenden Studenten den Ratschlag, sie auf dem Strich, die die beiden Werte abgrenzte, zu schreiben.[14]

Ich möchte wiederholen: Cardine glaubte bestimmt an die Möglichkeit, Werte *zu unterscheiden*, »obwohl nicht genau messbar sind, aufgrund ihrer natürlichen Ungenauigkeit«. Er glaubte an sie – ich hoffe, mich nicht zu irren – aufgrund einer strengen Methode, die, trotz seiner grossen Phantasie, ihn immer dazu trieb, rationale Fundamente in seinem Wirken zu suchen.

Es wird meiner Meinung nach Luigi Agustoni sein, der das Konzept der drei unterschiedlichen Werte fallen lässt, sicher nicht um die Elastizität der

---

12 J. CLAIRE, a.a.O. (Anm.1), S. 22.
13 Vgl. E. CARDINE, a.a.O. (Anm.7), S. 10.
14 Vgl. E. CARDINE, a.a.O. (Anm.2), S. 8 oder, in »Études Grégoriennes«, S. 10.

Noten zu annullieren, sondern um in einer im übrigen klaren Weise das Prinzip Kontext aufzustellen.[15]

Die *Semiologia Gregoriana* (1968) ist das grosse Werk, vor dem die wissenschaftliche Welt erstaunte. Sie ist von *Notes de cours* zusammengestellt, die Godehard Joppich und Rupert Fischer notiert haben. Ich konnte die Keimzelle der *Semiologia* bei Rupert Fischer sehen und feststellen, wie das Meisterwerk aus den Forschungen von Cardine entstand, die zu lebendigem Unterricht wurden.

Die *Semiologia* ist, wie bekannt, das Werk des radikalen Wendepunktes. Man muss hinzufügen, dass, seit dem Jahr 1958, am Päpstlichen Institut für Kirchenmusik Rom Magisteriumsthesen und Doktorarbeiten eingereicht wurden, die er von seinen Studenten entwickeln liess:[16]

1958 Paul Arbogast, *The small Punctum as isolated Note in Codex Laon 239* (»Études Grégoriennes«, III, 1959, S. 83–133);

1958 Thomas Gallen, *A Study of the Oriscus written* in prima manu *in Manuscript number 359 of the Library of Saint Gall;*

1959 René Ponchelet, *Les cadences finales des Graduels du IIIe mode du répertoire antique;*

+1959 René Ponchelet, *Les salicus du codex 359 de la Bibliothèque de Saint Gall dans la perspective de témoignage du codex 239 de Laon et du codex 47 de Chartres* (*Le salicus en composition dans le codex 359 de Saint Gall*, »Études Grégoriennes«, XIV, 1973, S. 7–125);

1959 Lawrence Heiman, *The Interpretation of the Neums significatively angular »in alto« found in the Cantatorium of Saint Gall 359;*

1960 Benvenuto Pugliese, *La strofa di apposizione nel Cantatorium di San Gallo 359;*

1961 Giles H. Pater, *The Use and the Meaning of the Episema on the last Part of the Porrectus in the Cantatorium St. Gall 359;*

1961 César Hilario, *El Torculus Resupinus en el Codice N° 121 de la Biblioteca de Einsiedeln;*

1962 Alberto Carotta, *Lo Scandicus con stacco dopo la seconda nota nel Cantatorium di San Gallo;*

1962 Walter Wiesli, *Der Pressus Maior und Minor und die Clivis in Apposition in den Kadenzformeln der Gradualien und Trakten;*

---

15 Vgl. L. AGUSTONI, *Esiste il valore medio nelle notazioni neumatiche gregoriane? Sul valore delle note e sulla teminologia*, »Studi Gregoriani«, IV, 1988, S. 21–27.

16 Ein kleines Kreuz vor dem Titel bedeutet Doktorarbeit. Im Fall von Veröffentlichung wird der Name der Zeitschrift oder der Titel des Buches unter Klammern angegeben.

1962 Columba Kelly, *Fr. Vollaert's two Exceptions to his general Rule of Length for the Laon 239 Virga. A Criticism*;

+1963 Walter Wiesli, *Die musikalische Funktion des Quilisma im Codex 359 von St. Gallen* (*Das Quilisma im Codex 359 der Stiftsbibliothek St. Gallen. Eine paläographisch-semiologische Studie*, Immensee 1966);

+1963 Columba Kelly, *The cursive Torculus Design in the Codex St. Gall 359 and its rhythmical Significance* (St. Meinrad, Indiana, 1964);

1964 Sebastià Bardolet, *Valor i caràcter del salicus a l'articulació sillàbica*;

1965 Camillo Dallafior, *Il torculus speciale nel manoscritto di Benevento* VI, 33;

1967 Claudio Moscatelli, *Il pes quadratus nello stacco neumatico nel codice 121 di Einsiedeln*;

+1967 William Jordan, *The Signs of Prolongation used in the Codex St. Gall 359 in certain Types of melodic Descents. A Nuance or double Time-value?*;

+1968 Claude Thompson, *La traduction mélodique du Trigon dans les pièces authentiques du Graduale Romanum* (»Études Grégoriennes«, X, 1969, S. 29–86, u. *Le trigon dans le codex 359 de St. Gall*, Trois Rivières [Canada], 1980).

Hier ist auf die Arbeiten Bezug genommen, die bis zum Jahr 1968 entstanden; andere, die später eingereicht wurden, waren sicher schon in Bearbeitung. Man kann auch sehen, dass alle diese Arbeiten, sowohl die grossen als auch die kleinen, wissenschaftliche Aspekte berührten, an die der Meister dachte.

Ich erinnere mich, als er mit mir über Arbogast sprach und über das kleine Punctum in Laon. Er sang es in den Intonationskontexten, von unten nach oben.

Man denke an die Magisteriumsthese von Thomas Gallen über den Oriscus: über dieses besondere Zeichen, das nicht unentbehrlich und doch insofern ausserordentlich ist, dass es als Einzelnote immer von einer niedrigeren gefolgt wird.

Als die Doktorarbeit von René Ponchelet über den Salicus in Komposition diskutiert wurde, sass ich unter den Zuhörern. Es war damals Direktor des Instituts der grosse Igini Anglés, eine echte Säule in einer guten Zeit des Instituts. Durch diese Dissertation wurde die alte Weise, das Zeichen zu sehen, nämlich mit der zweiten Note als der wichtigsten, revolutioniert: die wichtigste Note ist dagegen die dritte, die höchste.

Oder die Doktorarbeit von Walter Wiesli, die auch gegen die alte Meinung unanfechtbar bewies, dass das Ziel der Bewegung eines Quilisma-Scandicus die höchste Note ist, nicht die niedrigste, die sekundär ist.

Ebenfalls die Doktorarbeit eines sehr guten Schülers aus Australien, William Jordan, die bewies, wie es falsch war, die zwei unisonischen Noten in pressusähnlichen Kontexten als einen verdoppelten Ton zu betrachten und nicht voneinander unabhängig.

Man kann sehen, dass die Forschungen des Meisters und diejenigen, die er seinen Schülern auftrug, nur ein Ziel hatten: die Fundamente zu vertiefen und zu verbinden, die zu einer echten Grammatik führten, deren die Disziplin Bedarf hatte.

Diejenigen, die noch der Semiologie fern sind oder sie verachten, müssten überlegen. Sie ist Frucht genialer Intuitionen und genialer Forschungen und bildet die unentbehrliche Säule für die Analyse und die Interpretation, weil sie, wir möchten es wiederholen, wie die Grammatik für eine Sprache ist. In seinem schon erwähnten Testament definiert der Meister den Betrag der Schüler eine »kostbare Mitarbeit, die das Feld der Kenntnisse erweiterte und deren Fundiertheit bewies«.[17]

Der *Primo Anno di Canto Gregoriano*, ursprünglich in italienischer Sprache veröffentlicht, ist ein dem Anschein nach einfaches Werk, tatsächlich aber, aufgrund seiner ausserordentlichen Modernität und seiner Öffnung in die Zukunft, gewaltig angelegt. 1970, nach der *Semiologia*, veröffentlicht, ist dieses Buch in Wahrheit ihr Fundament, von der integrierenden Persönlichkeit Cardines beherrscht, der sofort beginnt, die neue Richtung festzulegen.

Anlässlich des Jubiläums von Trondheim habe ich das Werk wiedergelesen und, fast nach 30 Jahren, bin ich noch mehr von der Genialität seiner Anlage beeindruckt worden. Er entwickelt vom Anfang bis zum Ende im Grunde eine einzige Idee, sicher nicht neu, doch mit kräftigem Sinn der Modernität wieder aufgeworfen: die grundlegende Wichtigkeit des Textes und das unlösliche, besser konstitutionelle Verhältnis zwischen Text und Melodie (der Choral ist »parole chantée«[18]). Nie so etwas Kraftvolles gesehen.

Solch ein Bewusstsein der Konstitution des gregorianischen Chorals lässt das gut verstehen, was Jean Claire berichtet: »Ich habe Dom Cardine auf seinem Krankenbett mir am Ende einer tiefen Überlegung sagen hören: 'Ich hatte zwei Bücher geschrieben. Man hat sich auf das erst erschienene (die *Semiologia*) gestürzt, ohne auf das zweite (*Primo Anno*) aufmerksam zu sein, das dagegen wirklich die Basis von allem ist'«.[19]

---

17 Vgl. E. CARDINE, a.a.O. (Anm.2), S. 4 oder, in »Études Grégoriennes«, S. 5.
18 Vgl. E. CARDINE, *Première Année de Chant Grégorien*, franz. Ausgabe, Rome 1975, S. 33.
19 J. CLAIRE, a.a.O.(Anm.1), S. 21.

In der Tat setzt die *Semiologia* den anderen Text voraus. Dieser andere ist ein Werk, das die Wurzel in das Wesen des gregorianischen Gesanges steckt, und die *Semiologia* könnte ohne den *Primo Anno* irrtümlicherweise mit einem 'technischen', für jeden griffbereiten Werk verwechselt werden. Es handelt sich um eine wirkliche, feststellbare Gefahr. Ich persönlich verstehe gut die Behauptung von Jean Claire, der Cardine drastisch unter diejenigen einreiht, die den Text als das grosse Fundament des gregorianischen Repertoire betrachten: »Von dem historischen und logischen Vorstellen des Textes in Bezug auf die Melodie und von den einschlägigen Konsequenzen hat Dom Cardine gewollt, dass ein Beweis gerade im »technischen Vorwort« des künftigen *Antiphonale Romanum* gegeben wurde (*Liber Hymnarius*, Praenotanda, [. . . .], S.XVI). Solche Darstellung der Lesungsregeln einer verbesserten, ganz auf der Semiologie beruhenden Neumatik, endet mit dieser Erklärung, die das letzte Schlagwort sein möchte: 'Die in diesem Vorwort dargestellten Prinzipien kommen von einer vollkommenen Anpassung des heiligen Textes und der gregorianischen Melodie her. Daher besitzen schon diejenigen, die singen und sich bemühen, die lateinische Rezitation zu achten, das meiste, um den gregorianischen Gesang gut auszuführen'«.[20]

Und noch Jean Claire: »Die Semiologie steht im Dienst des Textes. Wenn das Wort und der Satz nicht durch die Bewegung der Akzentuierung gebaut sind, was nichts romantisches ist, sondern ein Bedürfnis existenzieller Logik, wird jede eventuell noch so wahre, echte, objektive semiologische Besonderheit, die zu diesem Mangel an Linie hinzugefügt wird, am Ziel vorbeiführen, und ihren richtigen Ausdruck nicht finden. Umsonst wird man sich an Berufssänger mit schönen Stimmen wenden: wenn sie den grundlegenden verbalen Stil nicht besitzen, werden ihre schönen Stimmen *gregoriano modo* nicht singen. Und es ist viel schwieriger, sie diesen grundlegenden verbalen Stil assimilieren zu lassen, als sie jede Besonderheit genauer Semiologie – Neumentrennung, Werte, Reperkussionen – zu unterrichten«.[21]

Als Dom Cardine versucht hat, Richtlinien für ein Programm gregorianischer Studien festzulegen, stellte er nach dem *Primo Anno* und der *Semiologie*, das Studium der Wort-Neume-Synthese, »die direkt zur Interpretation und zum Dirigieren führt«.[22] Wort-Neume-Synthese zu studieren heisst hier, diese Synthese zu vertiefen; besser gesagt, in ihrem tiefsten Wesen zu verstehen. »Danach könnte man einige Generalprinzipien präsentieren, die den Schülern erlauben,

---

20 *Ibidem*, S. 22.
21 *Ibidem*.
22 E. CARDINE, *Primo Anno di Canto Gregoriano*, Roma 1970, S. 64.